ADVANCE PRAISE

The future of innovation comes from collaborating employees who think differently and work toward a common goal. In this book, Priscilla nails the concept that proves that none of us can do it alone. She offers an amazing glimpse into a new way of thinking about how we should focus our efforts around teams.

—MICHAEL BRENNER, bestselling author of *Mean People Suck*

This simple mindset shift speeds up innovation, multiplies positive outcomes, and could even change our world.

—JON BOSTOCK, bestselling author of *The Elephant's Dilemma*

If you're not collaborating in sales and marketing today, your competition is already ahead of you. In this book, McKinney gets directly to the point on why collaboration has become the most important zeitgeist across leadership today. McKinney's book also will give you practical solutions that you can implement in your workplace and cascade through your teams.

—TIM HUGHES, bestselling author of *Social Selling*, Top 10 global influencer on Twitter and LinkedIn

For everyone who thinks that strategy is step one, open this book. You're about to discover that your own mindset is the foundation of any strategy. And they need to be in alignment. Priscilla has a new perspective for you that will change your approach to your marketing and your business. It's all right here.

We live in a world that is incredibly fluid; innovation is everywhere and can seem a daunting thing for us to deal with not just because everything is changing but because everything continues to change. Even our new ideas quickly become old, innovation becomes best practice, it's impossible to keep up. The answer is to find your dream team of people to work with—collaborating to innovate. Business and life become a constant brainstorm of ideas.

But without rules you have anarchy, so this collaboration needs its own rules too. The collaboration structure needs guidance, a rule book...and this book is it. A truly innovative look at how to innovate and a must for everyone in business.

In Collaboration Is the New Competition, *author and industry leader Priscilla McKinney shares her personal journey of embracing collaboration in the workplace and how it has transformed both her career and personal life. Through real-life examples and practical tips, she demonstrates how fostering a spirit of collaboration can lead to greater success and satisfaction in both your professional and personal endeavors. As a testament to her own successful approach, Priscilla has built a thriving digital marketing agency by bringing together diverse teams and cross-pollinating ideas, making her the perfect guide for readers looking to harness the power of collaboration for success.*

Author Priscilla McKinney perfectly embodies the principles she preaches in Collaboration Is the New Competition. *As a successful entrepreneur and owner of her own digital marketing agency, Priscilla has made a career out of collaboration and cross-pollination, bringing together diverse minds to achieve amazing results. In this book, Priscilla shares her secrets for fostering a collaborative environment and explains how these techniques can translate to success in every aspect of life. Buy this book if you want to see the power of collaboration in action.*

—WILLIAM LEACH,
bestselling author of *Marketing to Mindstates*

When I think of marketing, I think of Priscilla and this book as my #1 go-to. This book illuminates the story of how collaborating in our 24x7 world is essential for succeeding not just now but for the future. We can no longer play by the old rules when it comes to marketing. Priscilla's playbook plants the seeds for how to do things differently, adapt to rapidly changing industries and cultures, and set sail for future successes - while cultivating your mindset to get you to reach your dreams and goals. This is the marketing playbook we've desperately needed to not work smarter or harder, but to think differently - that is how we succeed in the next era of business.

—RACHAEL O'MEARA, Author of *Pause and Pause the Journal*, TEDx speaker and Executive Leadership Coach

COLLABORATION
IS THE NEW
COMPETITION

Tavia,
Here's to your next
big win through
collaboration.

COLLABORATION
IS THE NEW
COMPETITION

Why the Future of Work Rewards
a Cross-Pollinating Hive Mind
& How Not to Get Left Behind

PRISCILLA McKINNEY

Illustrations by Leighton Cordell

LIONCREST
PUBLISHING

COLLABORATION IS THE NEW COMPETITION

Why the Future of Work Rewards a Cross-Pollinating Hive Mind & How Not to Get Left Behind

Illustrations by Leighton Cordell

ISBN   978-1-5445-3543-2 *Hardcover*

         978-1-5445-3541-8 *Paperback*

         978-1-5445-3542-5 *Ebook*

For all of the quiet and unassuming acts of love that make my life insanely awesome and easier than it should be, I dedicate this book to The Steve.

Anyone who knows Steve expects this to be a full chapter, and it really should be. He is the pre-heater of my car, the chopper of the wood, the carrier of the water, the charcuterie board maker (even as I'm finishing up the last Zoom of the day), the Captain of 3LittleBirds, the headmaster of the McKinney homeschool, the daily vacuumer of the navy blue, velvet couch I insisted on buying, and of course, the famous homemade bread maker.

CONTENTS

INTRODUCTION

12 minute read

I CAN'T BELIEVE I WROTE A BUSINESS BOOK.

Thank goodness it's not a typical business book. I've read plenty of those, thinking I might glean some brilliant pearls of wisdom, but most business books are sad revisionist histories of some captain of industry's spectacular Cinderella story. In those stories, the protagonist has a plan right from the start and, despite the odds, does everything right to go from zero to hero with nary a misstep along the way.

We're told that getting to the top is simply a matter of an individual following a linear path, taking all the right steps, and climbing the proverbial ladder of success. Five secrets. Seven rules. Ten steps. Blech. It doesn't work that way, folks. Because there are no secrets, rules, or steps that guarantee success in business. You don't get from where you are now to where you want to be by following a neat little structure or plan, especially because those prescriptions are not applicable to many situations.

The books that have really changed my life did not offer me prescribed steps, but frameworks for change. They taught me how to perceive problems differently. They taught me to think differently. They taught me how to be disciplined in using these frameworks to give me a competitive advantage to moving from problem to solution more quickly and gracefully. Reflecting on this, I knew I didn't just *want* to write a business book, I *had* to.

This may not be the last business book the world ever needs, but it's the book the business world needs right now. Business has never been as simple, and it's never been more complicated than it is right now. So instead of serving up five secrets, seven rules, or ten steps, I'd like to invite you to think differently. Think critically. Be open to the possibility that there's another way to succeed in business, a better way to compete.

The bad news about this better way is that you can't do it alone. But the good news—the best news of all—is that you can't do it alone. Because succeeding in business isn't a one-way street. It isn't even a two-way street. It's a multi-lane highway with many vehicles coming and going all the time. Thinking otherwise, you might get a win here and there, sometimes even a win-win. But if you really want to compete, you're going to want to share the road.

How do I know? Experience.

It all started a few years ago, when I was invited to speak at a marketing research conference. The marketing research experts in attendance—my audience—were having trouble marketing their own businesses, so the event organizers wanted to bring in a fresh voice, someone outside their inner circle, to show them what they were missing.

At the time, with a degree in cultural anthropology, I understood enough about social science and research. Plus, as CEO of my own digital marketing company, I was an expert in digital marketing. But market research? That was beyond my scope of expertise. I wasn't sure if I was the right voice for the job, but never one to shy away from a speaking engagement (and an opportunity to broaden my network), I showed up, got on stage, and talked to that group of market researchers.

I didn't expect much of a response. Maybe some polite applause—and a request to never speak at a market research conference again. I was a hit. Not just a minor hit, but huge.

Like any other industry, people in market research had been hearing the same messaging and platitudes for years. They had been given the same solutions too. I was more than a breath of fresh air; I was someone from outside the industry who didn't accept the preconceived obstacles to their persistent and newly emerging challenges. Instead, I was deeply interested in listening to and learning about them. I was hearing about the challenges of marketing research with fresh ears and bringing fresh solutions to the party—er, conference.

My curiosity about market research companies was piqued. I learned everything I could about them and earned the right to pitch this industry my services.

The irony of the situation wasn't lost on me. Here were the top researchers in the country, people whose entire careers were predicated on understanding consumer behavior in order to improve how companies go to market with better marketing messages and better customer experiences. Yet these market researchers weren't doing market research on themselves, their brands, or their customers. And not only were they neglectful at doing *market research* on themselves, but they had also dropped the ball on *marketing* themselves.

This made no sense to me. By way of example, when I started my digital marketing business, Little Bird Marketing, I made my company my first customer. We had, and still have, ongoing marketing projects, and I apply the same rigor to their execution as I do to those of my top customers. It is my firm belief that the cobbler's kids should be wearing the best shoes in town.

Yet, time and time again market researchers tell me that they tried marketing and it didn't work, or they question why they should do research on their own brand. This is exactly what they expect their customers to do—why wouldn't they follow their own advice?

This was a turning point in my business and my career. Armed with what I knew about social science and research, and what I had learned about market research companies, I forged ahead—and seized the moment. I helped companies get unstuck from the past, discard their antiquated ways of marketing their businesses, and shift to a new way to solve problems and reach their most ideal customers.

It was a major shift for these companies. They had to learn how to compete in a way they had never considered: collaboration. I showed them how to get the right people in the room, who were often people they would never consider working with, sometimes even their own competition.

In today's world, each new challenge requires us to collaborate in a new way, with different players, different ideas, and different approaches. **Though collaboration isn't the answer for every business problem, it can be a powerful tool for getting ahead.** The future is full of collaboration. And not only do we need to collaborate in order to compete, we need to collaborate *properly*.

Most organizations follow pre-existing structures and rules, both spoken and unspoken. Nonprofits, for-profit companies, government organizations, and even our own families have a way of doing things. If you work within a company, you are aware of how things are done—the documented rules of engagement and the implied rules that everyone is supposed to know and follow to move forward in their career. We often take pride in the standard operating procedures.

But what if we operate within that structure and follow those rules and still don't move forward as quickly as we think we should? What if our progress is slow and painful, and our success limited?

We could step up our productivity by working faster, working longer, and adding more people to the team. That might work for factory and farm workers. But unless you're in the business of physical labor, that kind of work ethic isn't going to deliver the work- and life-changing results you want—or what the world needs. Work has changed, and for knowledge workers, working harder isn't the answer.

I am not proposing we work less. I am asserting that, within professional industries, doing more has a point of diminishing returns. It's time we acknowledged that task-driven work isn't the best way to solve our major non-task-driven problems.

So if working harder or smarter or working together aren't the best ways forward, what's left?

THINK A LITTLE HARDER, A LITTLE... DIFFERENTLY

What's left is thinking and working differently. Not differently the same way every time, but differently, *in a different way*, each time. We even have to think differently *about* thinking differently because there is no one solution to any challenge, problem, or goal. We need to engage deeply, using complex thinking to solve our deeply complex problems—the types of daily problems we are called upon to solve quickly.

If you see every problem merely as a series of tasks to complete, every goal as a series of tasks to accomplish, your results will be limited. What if we instead chose to view every challenge as an opportunity to manifest major wins? Not only individual wins, but also wins beyond ourselves and our organizations: wins for our industries, our communities, and the world.

This is only possible through collaboration. As knowledge workers, we *have to* collaborate. Even the smartest person in the room is limited in their intelligence, their creativity, and their experience. We have to move beyond the construct of maximizing individual effort.

However, I'm not saying we should collaborate for the sake of collaboration, and not even necessarily for the sake of diversity, inclusion, or the ever-popular idea of "bringing more people to the table." As a Hispanic woman, I love having my voice heard, but my voice isn't always the right one for the problem. Inviting a Black Millennial woman, an Asian Baby Boomer male, and a Generation Alpha non-binary individual to the table isn't necessarily the answer. That sounds like the perfect dinner party to me, but when it comes to collaboration, we need to invite the right people for the right reasons, with an agenda and with intention.

When you make that mindshift, you realize that collaboration—done right—*is* the new competition. Bigger wins come from those who effectively collaborate. The future of work rewards a cross-pollinating hive mind approach. As more realize this competitive advantage, it will become harder and harder to succeed any other way.

To compete, you need to understand the new structure and ground rules:

Everyone must have something to gain and something to lose. They must be willing to reveal their agendas. And they must have a strong desire to compete and win, not only for themselves, but for everyone at the table—and sometimes for people who aren't even in the room.

If this sounds more strategic than the typical, operational way of solving problems, it is—but not initially. A mindset shift must come first. Because moving straight to strategy is part of the problem. That immediate strategy that everyone's mind jumps to may not be the best strategy, especially if it's coming from the same person or the same group of people every time. The best strategy for this problem isn't necessarily the same strategy that worked for another problem that we solved last week or last year. Those strategies don't consider what's changed. They don't consider new players, new information, new technologies, new challenges, or most importantly, new opportunities for greater wins.

The very nature of strategy, by design, is limited and limiting. Strategy brings focus, but before we narrow our focus, let's make sure we're focusing on the right thing. Let's make sure we're looking outside the usual path to a solution. Are we going too narrow, with the people involved in the strategy and the potential beneficiaries of the outcome? Or are we excluding potentially more visionary minds and more informed voices, while neglecting the bigger wins? For those who are excluded from the process and the solution, that kind of strategy can be offensive. For those who are involved, that short-sightedness can be opportunity lost.

Collaboration done right, by contrast, is expansive. It begins before we even know who the players are, and it extends beyond them. It means making a commitment to discovering who the players are and also looking for who the winners might be beyond ourselves and our businesses. Collaboration is the process through which, over time, a better strategy organically appears. A strategy *will* appear, and probably a better one than one that's imposed upon the process or forced upon the players.

No one system will solve all of our problems. There is not one business book that offers the key to success, so that's not my intention here. In this book, I will give you a new way of looking at and engaging with collaboration, along with a number of tools or "anchors" that can help you think differently for better solutions and bigger wins. Because you may *think* you've tried collaboration before, but it's possible you haven't. Are you ready for the mindset shift?

WHAT DO I KNOW?

So, what do I know that everyone else doesn't?

My beliefs and methods around collaboration and competition weren't taught to me in college. I didn't learn them in a training course. Looking at problems from different angles is a skill I developed early in life.

The youngest of five girls, I traveled the world with my sisters as performers. We wore matching dresses, did puppet shows, and sang. There were a lot of road trips. I've lived in five states and thirty-three houses, and I attended four high schools in three countries.

Living in all those places instilled in me a curiosity about life, people, culture, and the interconnectedness of it all. I also developed an ability to accept and adapt to changes quickly. These are skills that served me in my own life, and in my career at the intersection of marketing, business, and market research.

In addition, I'm intrigued by human behavior, especially the emotional aspects that so often we seek to explain logically. I don't shy away from asking the hard questions or trying to answer them. Here's the most important thing I've learned by asking those questions—**collaboration is about leveraging the power of the hive mind, not relying on groupthink.**

Everyone knows that there's a queen in every beehive, but not everyone knows that different bees are DNA-coded to perform unique roles. Each bee independently contributes to the larger project: collecting honey. There is hierarchy, but each role is valued.

In groupthink, there's the illusion of freedom from hierarchy, but the truth is that everyone's unique skills are lost in the effort to conform. As a CEO, I have to be careful about choosing collaborators who have different experiences and opinions that are necessary for a project; otherwise, because of the natural functions of hierarchy, my voice will dominate the room and the project will suffer.

There is a hierarchy in every relationship. Collaborating isn't about removing hierarchy; it's about not letting hierarchy designate the value of the contribution being made.

In addition, everyone participating should have something to gain or lose. For example, if you wanted to address the problem of homelessness in your city, you might gather four CEOs from businesses downtown, the Director of Health and Human Services from the local hospital, and three people from a nonprofit. But you should also consider the end user. **How can you collaborate on the most effective solution to end homelessness without inviting homeless people to the conversation?**

If you want to solve wicked problems, you need to bring the right people to the table and engage the hive mind. When you do this, you'll recognize that you have so much more to give than you might expect and that others are willing to give back to you in return.

The hive mind approach to collaboration goes a step further than the Golden Rule, which asks you to treat others the way you want to be treated. It involves the Platinum Rule, which asks you to treat others as *they* want to be treated. In this buzzing hive, someone might not be able to help, but they definitely know someone who can. When they see how you're willing to give and create bigger solutions for everyone in the room, they're more than willing to be a part of that win-win-win-win. Everyone comes together to create huge wins: your friends, your friends' friends, and your friends' friends' friends... you get the point.

When you see yourself reflected in others—in your colleagues, your customers, and even in your competitors—and don't treat them like obstacles to overcome in order to make a sale, you can get the full benefit of that connection and create some pretty great relationships along the way.

A MENTAL WORKOUT

Collaboration is the New Competition isn't a step-by-step guide to take you from business disaster to business success. It's a mental workout of sorts to help you think differently about how you do business.

Just thinking differently is the start. In part one, "Setting Sail," I'll describe the mindset shift that will help you see collaboration in a way you've never seen it before, including why your previous experiences weren't collaboration, what true collaboration looks like, and why it's the new competition. Once you've made this mindset shift and seen the world with fresh eyes, you can't unsee it. When you get there, the old way of doing things will seem strange and obsolete.

Think of this book as a pattern interrupt. It's a brief reprieve from the way you've been doing business, but it contains a powerful idea that you can put to work immediately. When you act on the concept of collaboration as the new competition, you begin to reset your own patterns of behavior and enlist interrupts that will change outcomes.

You'll need tools to take action—to put your new thinking to work. Part two of this book, "Casting Anchors," is a toolkit packed with specific ways of looking at problems and alternate ways to solve them. I call these anchors, and I gave each one a sticky title to make it memorable, so when you're struggling with an issue, an anchor might occur to you as another plan of attack that you hadn't considered.

You're busy, and I'm busy too. Though we have to make time to think and to learn, I understand you don't have time for lengthy epics. With this in mind, I've kept each chapter—including the anchors—to a nice tight read that you can finish in eight to twelve minutes (at an average of 238 words per minute).[1]

Collaboration as the new competition means thinking differently about winning, and surprise—it starts the same way many great stories begin: *A man walks into a bar...*

---

1   Marc Brysbaert, "How many words do we read per minute? A review and meta-analysis of reading rate," *Journal of Memory and Language*, December 2019

Part One

SETTING SAIL

"A ship in harbor is safe—but that is not what ships are built for."

— JOHN A. SHEDD

I LOVE A GOOD NAUTICAL THEME, BUT MORE THAN ANYTHING I love the freedom inherent in setting sail. I chose this metaphor for part one because you must choose to leave the harbor and sail into the unknown. No matter how many times you leave the same anchorage, you always see things differently. No two journeys at sea are the same. That is what I'm asking you to do: let go of the line and venture out to see something new.

Part one is the what and the why of collaboration. Why am I asking you to make a mindset shift, to think of collaboration as the new competition? What does that even mean?

You're about to find out.

Once you start thinking in a different way, you'll never be able to unsee or unlearn what you've encountered in this book—and it will be life changing. When you have a new perspective, you open yourself to abundance beyond what you can attract on your own.

We begin by interrupting our normal pattern of thinking and perceiving and creating. This book will let you step away from how you've always done things. In that reprieve, you can make the change that puts you on a better trajectory—and serves as a wakeup call for others.

FORGET THE BLONDE

8 minute read

A MAN WALKS INTO A BAR... AND THAT MAN IS RUSSELL CROWE. Well, Russell Crowe's character John Nash in *A Beautiful Mind*.

John Nash, a mathematician and game theorist, is out for drinks with his friends when a beautiful blonde and her friends enter the bar. Nash's companions crowd around him, each man planning how they're going to approach the blonde. One of his friends quotes famed 18th century economist Adam Smith: "In competition, individual ambition serves the common good."

Nash has an epiphany. "Adam Smith needs some revision," he says. "If we all go for the blonde, we block each other."

He realizes that if it's every man for himself, the blonde will reject them all—as will her friends, who won't like being second choice. But, if they forget the blonde and go for the other girls, who are used to being ignored in favor of their friend, they all end up with a date. The only way that everyone wins is by doing what's best for themselves *and* for the group.

Excited to develop his theory, Nash rushes out of the bar and stops to thank the very confused blonde who has no idea she inspired a major development in game theory.

PRIORITIZE THE LONG GAME

At the core of Nash's plan was collaboration: bringing together the opposing values of the men and women to find the best outcome for the most people. The guys all aimed for the blonde because she was the most attractive, but she was operating by a different system. She would have turned them all down because she valued her friends, who would have felt inferior being the clear second choice. Nash found the commonality in which the most people got a date: everyone *except* the blonde. (But, if the blonde truly valued her friends' feelings, then she didn't necessarily lose, did she?)

If all parties want the same thing, as long as there's a change in the way they go about it, they can likely all achieve what they want. When all collaborators understand each other's operating systems, everyone suspends their own modus operandi to achieve the desired outcome. It's prioritizing the long game over a short-sighted win: everyone can still get what they want, but they might have to get there differently. And, even if there are a few who don't get exactly what they want, everyone gets more of what they want than they would have had they not collaborated. Collaboration allows for more complex, nuanced wins.

Everyone has ambition. To be their best—to be *the* best. It's natural, and it's what makes strong leaders. But when everyone is too focused on beating their competitors, no one can break out of the vicious individualistic cycle and reach their full potential. The only way that nobody loses and everyone wins is to forget the blonde.

From Competitor to Collaborator

A competitor measures their limited success by that of others. A collaborator measures success objectively.

When a collaborator walks into a bar—or a meeting, a conference, or anywhere else that people gather for a common cause—they look around and ask, "What does everyone need? What's the greater good?" Collaborators understand that the greater good feeds off abundance. This fundamental mindset shift is essential to understanding the power of collaboration. It's impossible to get a different outcome without first taking a different approach.

To benefit from "forgetting the blonde," each participant has to abandon the competitor mindset and embrace the collaboration mindset. That means not falling for the scarcity scam that is perpetuated by the competition model. Collaboration works on a very different premise: a belief in abundance. The truth is, there's already enough for everyone—and there's *more* than enough when we lift each other up and go far beyond what each of us can do on our own.

Disrupt the status quo. Escape the winners-versus-losers trap and embrace abundance.

A Man Walks into a Career...

Here's what the old way of thinking gets you:

A man walks into a career. Before he even takes his seat at the table, he surveys the room and automatically sees scarcity. He believes that there's a limited well of success and promotions that will dry up if he doesn't drain it first. If he wins, somebody else is going to have to lose.

All of these things aren't true, and yet that's the pervasive mindset in business. Our willing participation makes us complicit in its continued, outdated, inefficient, and destructive existence.

Somewhere in business history, we agreed to meeting structures where the most senior people talk first and everyone else is lucky to squeeze in a word. We value attribution over ideas, focusing on the person who brings an idea forward rather than its benefit, a practice that encourages people to claim credit for other people's work. When missteps occur in this individualized structure, failure also is assigned to an individual. The blame game begins.

What kind of environment does this create for people who are supposed to be solving problems? It creates an environment filled with organization silos, distrust, and paranoia. It's distracting. It's tiring. We're looking over our shoulders for the inevitable knife in the back. *Et tu, Brute?*

Unless we trust everyone in the room, we do not reveal what we really want. We hide our ambitions and agendas, assuming that letting others know what we're after sets us up as easy targets and leaves us vulnerable to attack. Vulnerable to the competition that's going to swoop in and grab the scarce resources that we want.

We all have agendas, but hiding them away like dirty little secrets doesn't help us. We clutch them to our chests like prized cards in a poker game... and we leave the room empty-handed.

What if all of the cards were on the table?

Laying it out for all the players to see—revealing your piece of the puzzle—can be scary, especially if you're clinging to a scarcity mindset. But doing so changes the game; it turns that poker game with only one winner into a jigsaw puzzle where, piece by piece, a bigger vista is revealed. In this scenario, each person has a different piece, and you need all of them to complete the puzzle and produce a complete picture.

But you have to show your piece. You have to be clear and honest about what you have and what you want. Otherwise, you will never see the other pieces and not only will you never see the finished puzzle, *no one* will see the whole thing—the big picture of wins that are possible when everyone collaborates will remain invisible to all.

Everybody wants to go home with somebody at the bar. The sooner you admit that to yourself and the people on your team— or in any group where there's an opportunity for collaboration— the sooner you will discover a solution that benefits everyone.

Throughout this book, I'll talk about how this mentality presents itself in our careers, companies, and communities so that we can work toward a more collaborative and successful environment for everyone.

Forgetting the blonde and adopting an abundance mindset gets easier the more you do it. Start practicing this week. For inspiration, check out the following examples, then create your own.

A CLOSER LOOK: THE FIGHT CLUB OF THE INSIGHTS INDUSTRY

Ryan Barry, President of Zappi, is a great model of a leader who knows how to collaborate for bigger wins.

Historically, the corporate environment where Ryan lives is one of deep competition, one that may even be described as bordering on secrecy. And there are great reasons why it should. Zappi provides a unique technology and methodology for meaningful consumer feedback in order to create inspired marketing and advertising. They have honed the gathering of consumer insights process so creators can focus on delivering really tight brands, on point messaging and creative, and better-than-average product experiences. But in 2017, when they decided to make a significant pivot in the market, they decided to not go it alone.

Ryan understands that great collaboration doesn't involve divulging trade secrets. He knows there can be an exchange of ideas, mindsets and lessons learned at a very high level, improving work within an industry vertical and even crossing the aisle to another vertical so that new thoughts can be applied to tough challenges.

The traditional way forward would be to speak privately with leading Consumer Insights professionals at McDonald's, Coca-Cola and the like. Zappi could build the platform out with direct feedback from these super users, but Ryan and the team dreamed a bigger dream, placing their full bet on the brands already using their platform. This strategy would almost certainly create an overnight loss of about 30% of their revenue, but the wins could be exponential.

With the mindset that the wins would not just be for Zappi, Ryan selected a few high-level clients who were interested in coming together in a circle of trust to meet regularly and share their challenges, learnings, needs and more. Each seasoned and respected member would have something to lose and something to gain, would be willing to put their agendas on the table (not trade secrets), and would pursue the collaboration with a drive to win for themselves, for their brands, for Zappi, and for the others in the group. The Insights Alliance was born.

This group now meets regularly to give these brands exactly what they want from the platform and more. In this collaboration, exponential learnings are made for many brands, Zappi gets the feedback to improve their product (and the admiration of their best clients for out-of-the-box thinking), and here's the clincher—consumers are winning too. When you have brands who can learn from each other about how best to listen to the consumer, a deeper co-creation can happen. That is a better world for us all.

Insights Alliance is a fight club of sorts, and if you ask me about it in public I'm going to have to deny its existence. But significant begging allowed me to share this collaborative approach and showcase this thought leadership in action. I hope Zappi's example inspires you to look at non-traditional approaches to work and consider how collaboration could be a game changer.

DON'T LET THE VULTURES GET YOU DOWN

It's hard to break away from life-long scarcity brainwashing, especially when you aren't even conscious of it. Even the most generous people can be unintentionally warped by scarcity beliefs, so it will take work to push through and find the best way forward. But it's worth it. After all, many people told Ryan his idea was dumb and doomed.

Even with cautious optimism, clashing agendas can undo the best intentions of collaboration. If just one man in that scene from *A Beautiful Mind* had eyes for only the blonde, Nash's plan probably wouldn't have worked. He could've shared his true agenda and worked with the others to create another solution, but if he were operating from a scarcity mindset and kept his agenda to himself, he also could've used the plan to his advantage to get the blonde himself, ruining the outcome for everyone else.

Seeking out the right people for a collaborative endeavor takes time and patience. Some people will enter collaboration, pull a bait-and-switch, and go for the blonde. These vultures are likely already conducting business without good faith and their reputation has gotten around.

If someone is reticent about sharing their agenda, they're not a reliable collaborator. But remember, the street goes (at least) two ways. Withholding your personal agenda, even out of a sense of social niceties and a fear of being rude, is teaching others that they can't share their agendas in turn.

I fully believe in the power of collaboration, but I'm not going to walk into a bar I don't know with people I don't trust. Get picky about the bars you frequent—and the people with whom you frequent them. Set a standard for creating boundaries and relating with others so that you can build collaboration together.

FROM WIN-LOSE TO EXPONENTIAL WINS

12 minute read

IF ONLY ALL PROBLEMS WERE AS SIMPLE TO SOLVE AS GETTING a date at the bar. Take sustainability, for example: it's a complex problem that has to be addressed with multi-faceted solutions from many different groups and individuals.

Is it any surprise that we continue to struggle with a problem as simple as waste reduction when, since the 1960s, America's approach to sustainability has been centered only on the individual? Each of us is told to reduce, reuse, and recycle. How many people among the hundreds of millions of US residents are actually willing to do that if it takes a lot of time and effort?

This individual effort is possible in places like Orange County, Southern California, where people can toss everything into the trash and know that it will be sorted and recycled because of an intricate waste management system. But in most areas in the US, people have to sort their trash before they put it on the curb, making individual efforts toward sustainability much less accessible. In my household, we sort everything ourselves, drive to the nearest recycling center—which is in another city and, in fact, a different state—and put our recyclables into each bin by hand. We are clearly an anomaly for this community.

The message of reduce, reuse, recycle sounds good, but when it's a one-way street, there aren't many wins happening. Sustainability is clearly not being addressed by this individual-only approach. There can't be a win-win situation when the responsibility is on the individual only.

Business used to be a one-way street from business to consumer; businesses provided goods and services, and customers accepted them. Then, thanks to the internet, social media, and online reviews, it became a two-way street.

Consumers had plenty to say about their wants and needs, and companies were forced to listen if they wanted to compete.

That corner bar where people had to forget the blonde if they all wanted to win is now a sprawling nightclub and everyone in it has an agenda. An astute company sees this not as a challenge but as an opportunity. They can create a big win for themselves, as well as wins for their customers, by tackling problems more collaboratively.

In the corporate world, the fancy name for this is "co-creation." It is the idea that complex challenges can be addressed by involving consumers, acknowledging the humanity of the people in charge of the brands and the humanity of those consuming the products. It is a mindset dissolving that line between company and consumer, finding a better way forward for all humans. Whatever you call it, just get started.

It's up to us to find the right people—the businesses, industry leaders, partners, vendors, customers, colleagues, and more—with whom to collaborate for the biggest wins for ourselves, for others, and sometimes, for the world.

STRUCTURING MULTILAYERED WINS

Big, multilayered wins are easy when the agendas of all parties are aligned, but it's usually not so simple. At first glance, everyone's agendas may appear to have nothing in common or be in direct competition. To find common ground, you must acknowledge the existence of competing, and oftentimes hidden, agendas and then seek out any commonalities. From there, the negotiations begin.

Getting to the truth of "what everyone wants," however, is difficult. Companies want to make a profit. Customers don't want to contribute more of their own money to that profit. Everyone wants to do the ethical thing. Until each party is willing to own up to what they really want, even when it conflicts with what others want, collaborating to find a solution is an exercise in futility.

If you ask a consumer leaving a store why they bought a certain product, they might say they bought it because it's good for the environment. Maybe the packaging is recyclable or reusable. In market research, this is called "self-reporting." Self-reporting might provide a truth, but it probably doesn't tell the whole truth.

The consumer may have bought the product because it was less expensive, or it was on sale, or it came in a convenient size or package. The fact that it was also environmentally friendly may have differentiated it from other products and may have been a consideration in the buyer's mind, but it probably wasn't the deciding factor. If that same consumer went back to the store and the product wasn't on sale, would they still buy the eco-conscious product or reach for one that is cheaper and less sustainable? Because the self-reporting system prioritizes one value or another, consumers aren't allowed to be honest with themselves or with their reporting as to their buying decisions. The results are naturally skewed.

Behavioral scientists who deal with consumer insights and shopper behavior say that market research shows that sustainability is a big issue for consumers. They also agree that the subject is more complex than wanting to save the earth on an individual level. Using self-reported market research alone to validate an assumption that consumers will automatically choose sustainable products over similar, unsustainable ones is misguided. We must also consider other factors, such as cost and convenience.

Unfortunately, traditional market research often doesn't allow for consumers' competing values and priorities. For example, if you are asked, "Would you like to buy the eco-friendly XYZ product?" you would most likely answer, "Yes." A survey that asks for a Yes/No response or that asks people to self-report the reason they made their purchase assumes there was ONE reason why they bought the product and also assumes the consumer was aware of the bigger WHY behind their action. Forcing people to choose one answer over another creates a win-lose situation for the individual, never mind hopeful collaborators. If instead the question was asked "Would you buy the eco-friendly XYZ product if it costs 40% more?" you would begin to understand competing values. In fact, research has shown that only a fraction of consumers are willing to pay more for a product that is environmentally safe.[2]

Relying on research with a limited view of competing values, companies are blind to how complex the stories consumers tell themselves are. We rarely buy a product for one, clear reason. The fact is that we all have hidden narratives we may not even be conscious of, and when brands fail to address this complexity, they miss out on opportunities to connect deeply with shoppers' spoken and unspoken needs.

Consumers might feel guilty about sacrificing one value for another, but only for a moment. After all, how are they supposed to do the right thing for their families and for the planet when companies aren't giving them products that deliver that win-win? To further complicate the matter, consumers are demanding companies take the onus for sustainability. They want businesses to figure out what's most sustainable and offer it at a comparable price to other products. They will argue that companies decide what to put on store shelves, not consumers. On the other side of the argument, companies argue that what's environmentally friendly

---

2 https://explorerresearch.com/2022-retrospective-top-sustainability-trends/

is going to cost more, and if they put it on the shelves, there is no guarantee that shoppers will want to pay for it.

These conflicting bodies have the same end goal: products that meet the consumer's desires. Companies can deal with these conflicting values by structuring a larger deal. If they truly understand all the hidden agendas, figure out what is preventing them from meeting all of these desires, and solve that problem, they will create more wins for everyone. They can begin the process with story hearing.

Story Hearing

I love the concept of "story hearing" from Leigh Caldwell at Irrational Agency.[3] Instead of asking simple questions about complex problems, their methodologies invite consumers to share stories, which include memories, emotions and imaginative future outcomes. This qualitative listening exposes hidden narratives that even they may not be aware of. The practice can facilitate structuring bigger wins because it allows for more than one answer about why someone did what they did.

It's impossible to isolate one answer because *there is no one answer.*

---

3 https://blog.irrationalagency.com/storytelling-requires-story-hearing-why-customer-narratives-matter

It's not a bad thing for a mom who is trying to stretch her dollar to say, "I would love to help the environment, but this cleaner is $2.50 cheaper, and that's what I have to choose." Asking her to choose between A or B is not an accurate reflection of her agenda because it doesn't reflect her values *and* circumstances. To truly understand her, you have to be willing to listen to more than one layer of the story at a time.

There are larger problems to solve than just yours, mine, or anyone else's, but no one person can solve them alone. Because story hearing combats the win-lose structure in traditional methods of market research, I challenge market researchers to scrutinize how they are structuring consumer opinion polls, quantitative surveys, qualitative research, and behavioral analysis, ensuring that they are allowing for the inherent complexity of people.

What if corporations took the same approach? How much good could we unleash if large organizations pooled their resources to structure larger wins? We all know that sustainability is important in securing a brighter future, but we won't get any closer to figuring out how we can all win more if we aren't willing to collaborate and truly listen to each other. If only we could all lay our cards on the table and reveal our hidden agendas. Imagine the possibilities.

What we can learn from this innovative approach to behavioral science can also be applied to any challenge we're trying to solve through collaboration. Asking a simple question of those collaborating will yield a simple answer—a truth. But it will not be the whole truth. Instead, we can acknowledge competing values, multiple agendas (even ones we're not fully aware we walked into the room with) and more when we leave behind a binary win-lose mindset and embrace a more complex set of truths from which to frame the collaboration.

DISRUPTING THE STATUS QUO

To be considered the best of the best today, companies can't just come out with the best product, even if that results in a win-win for company and customer. Consumers no longer say, "Thanks for the great cleaning product!" and move on; today, they demand that brands operate within the consumer's values or at least make a stand and showcase their own values. Wins that resonate with today's consumer include values reflecting sustainability, employee satisfaction, customer experience, and diversity and inclusion. In short, their demands are complex.

Companies have to listen to what consumers want *and* who else they can get into the winner's circle. If you have the best product, but aren't winning for anyone else, you'll lose. Best of the best brands have moved beyond the binary view of "I win, you lose," to embrace a new truth: "many of us must win in order for me to win."

Consumers wanted to save the planet in theory, but they really wanted manufacturers to do better. A collaboration was required. Instead, you must also be able to say something like, "I make a great product that assuages your guilt about the environment, you buy more of it, and the environment wins." Even better if your brand also provides a kickback to the consumer's local school system. Everybody wins.

Consider the shift in the electric vehicle (EV) market since it started. At the beginning of electric vehicle technology, producing an energy efficient EV actually used more energy than a gas-powered one because the parts were sourced from around the world. The carbon footprint was greater than the environmental advantages. However, as the technology has matured, the carbon footprint of electric vehicles has decreased significantly.

Consumers wanted EVs, but they wanted manufacturers to do better. No one company could do that single-handedly, but as demand increased, more companies entered the market, lowering the energy cost per vehicle and the overall footprint of EV production. Companies were forced into the market by consumer demand for the product, but they were able to make a profit and satisfy the environmental demands of the public only because so many companies made this switch. More wins meant more business.

Structuring more wins is exciting. We don't know what's possible until we investigate and do it. Uncovering more avenues for disruption and more wins for more people, more companies, and more communities, we can change the world.

By embracing a win-win-win mindset, Uber introduced ride sharing, connecting people with cars, free time, and a desire for more income. They disrupted the transportation industry by leveraging app technology, as well as the agendas of tech investors and commuters who wanted to know what their ride would cost before they reached their destination or even agreed to get in the car. No New York City cabbie thought any of this was possible, but it was—once someone made the mindset shift.

Everyday activities that we take for granted as unchangeable are not only changeable, they can and are being changed. In some cases, they're being upended.

Clearing the Hurdles

These stories are familiar to most of us now, and we file them under the "disruption" tab in our minds. But I'm here to tell you disruption isn't enough. And it's risky. Many times, companies don't have the infrastructure or resources to keep products on the shelf or even create them.

The high cost and financial risk of a startup is what prevents many companies from becoming disruptors. Companies need more—more information, more help, more resources. They need to coordinate logistics, the archaic system of supply chain, people working on docks, and long-haul truck drivers who are underpaid and away from families.

They also need to understand how hard it is to change consumer behavior. As humans, we want things to stay the same emotionally and psychologically. Even though a new technology might be amazing, there's no guarantee that people are going to buy into what you made. The public has to be reeducated to buy the new product.

Sometimes the reeducation happens organically—my parents are now on Zoom, but that's only because the COVID-19 pandemic necessitated that people adopt new technology they normally wouldn't have used. Had Zoom followed the normal course of latency of adoption, it wouldn't have been a disruptor in communication. You can't always rely on a global pandemic to accelerate adoption.

If you do conquer huge startup costs and the difficulty of behavioral change, you'll still face that old nemesis: competition. As you're trying to disrupt an industry, someone else is trying to disrupt the same industry—and they may disrupt it better than you. For example, Uber opened the door for Lyft, which is now their biggest rival.

Or consider video streaming. When HBO created their own streaming service, they weren't going to have as many people opting for that channel on cable. But consumers had spoken: they wanted streaming. If HBO hadn't provided a streaming service, eventually their customers would have left completely in favor of other streaming services. If you don't move forward, the world isn't going to stand still for you—after all, when was the last time you stepped into a Blockbuster to pay a late fee? Or held a Nokia phone?

The corporate graveyard is filled with obsolete companies like Nokia, Blockbuster, Sears, Kmart and Bed, Bath and Beyond—companies that failed to listen to what consumers wanted. They refused to see a bigger picture of who could win and what could change, and the world shifted from underneath them until they could no longer stand.

Don't let your company's name end up on a tombstone—seek out all of the wins.

A CLOSER LOOK: ALL THE WINS

This is what Truman's, the eco-friendly cleaning product company, did. They understood that consumers want to help the environment, but only if they can do it at a price point that fits their budget.

Truman's considered consumers' demands for sustainability, combined with the wide-spread issues of the water crisis and the global shipping-container crisis, and asked, "Why are we shipping bottles of water around the world?" Then, the company focused on one thing and one thing only: resource-conscious products that satisfied consumers. Instead of putting another big plastic bottle of cleaner on store shelves, the company introduced refillable containers and a subscription service of cost-effective, environmentally friendly cleaning products to fill them. They gave customers a new choice in cleaning with convenient, affordable, guilt-free products.

The move wasn't only a win for the consumer. Because transportation and resource costs were cut, retailers won. Truman's won too, because they no longer had to manufacture a new bottle for every product sold; the refills took up less space, so their storage and shipping costs were reduced; and the subscription model allowed them to better predict sales. The company won, consumers won, retailers won, and *the environment* won—all because Truman's looked for those opportunities.

Ultimately, Truman's was bought by a larger company that increased distribution, and their model became widely adopted by consumers, influencing competitors and businesses in other industries. Now everyone is selling products without the water included, such as cleaning pellets, dissolvable laundry sheets, and container-free shampoo.

By combining ingenious marketing with a disruptive production and distribution model that created multilayered wins, Truman's had an impact far beyond even the cleaning industry. Win, win, win, win, win.

A BIGGER PODIUM

The model of competition has long been the one-on-one contest, which leaves no room for collaboration. Only one Olympian per competition could take home the gold. Collaboration, however, widens the podium so there can be more winners. Multiple people, businesses, organizations, and even global crises like water and container shortages can take home a gold medal.

When collaboration is at its peak, you multiply wins beyond what you can achieve alone. Because Truman's was willing to engage with consumers' competing agendas, they found the solution that benefited everyone and disrupted an entire industry, all while creating major wins for sustainability.

All these wins sound great, right? You're probably wondering why everyone isn't collaborating. Well, it's not always as easy as it sounds. Let's take a look at what collaboration is not.

3

REDEFINING COLLABORATION

7 minute read

WHEN ONE OF MY SONS WAS IN FIFTH GRADE, HE HAD TO DO A large group project for science class. An independent worker, my son already disliked group projects and asked his teacher why everyone was collaborating instead of doing individual work. His teacher couldn't answer the question. It seemed they were "collaborating" for collaboration's sake; there was no clear purpose or goal.

There were five students in my son's project group, and in theory the work was supposed to be split evenly between them. Ultimately, however, my son did the lion's share of the work. Because he had to communicate with the other four people—and deal with the unpredictability of what they committed to doing versus what they actually completed—the project took more time and effort than if he had done it himself.

From school kids to CEOs, we all get forced to "collaborate" at some point. The process seldom benefits everyone—especially the unlucky person who takes on most of the project. With no ground rules or accountability, one or a few people end up overworked, while everyone else reaps the benefits. Sometimes, when no one steps up, or when people who would typically step up get disgusted with the model, the project implodes in an unproductive debacle.

I believe the model is well-intended: somewhere along the line, someone actually believed that, in every situation, more hands made lighter work. In reality, that's rarely the case.

True collaboration engages the hive mind, relying on the collection of individual contributions to create better outcomes for everyone. The star player or the smartest kid in the group has to believe that instead of having much to lose, they have much to gain; they can come out a winner, and *all* the players, whatever their contribution, can come out winners too.

Still, we learn the flawed "collaboration" model in our formative years, and it continues to impact us in formalized systems at our companies. We need to agree that this model *is not* collaboration. If you're fifty years old and group projects make you feel like you're back in the fifth grade, that's a dead giveaway that what you're being asked to do is not collaborative.

FAILED ATTEMPTS AT COLLABORATION

In theory, when people work together, the work is more efficient. However, group projects often fall apart. Everyone "collaborated," but to what end? Time was wasted, nothing was resolved, and the project wasn't completed. If it was completed, it wasn't completed as well as it could have been, or as early as it should have been, and someone—the person who did most of the work—isn't happy. People involved in poorly crafted collaborations come to see them as nuisances that suffer from groupthink and prolong the work cycle, disrupting the team's culture and accomplishing less in more time.

Let's look more specifically at how groupthink causes collaboration attempts to fail.

Groupthink Doesn't Consider the Individual

Collaboration for the sake of collaboration overlooks each individual's core skills. It obscures the best way for the people in the room to work together. It demotivates the team's star players because they do most of the work and never get their deserved credit. They resent their team and think that they might as well have worked independently to create the outcome faster than wasting time delegating responsibility and following up on subpar work and missed deadlines.

When these star players are consistently taken advantage of, they can become impatient, commandeer the entire project, and force everyone in the group to do things their way. This is groupthink: when a power imbalance doesn't create space for people to share ideas. Team members with meaningful input who haven't been given a chance to shine are left on the sidelines, and the best solutions and ideas are buried because the same people always take charge. (Those who take charge are not always the star players, by the way. They may very well be the loudest or most opinionated.)

Forced collaboration doesn't consider people's skills, and it also doesn't create the structure for how those skills might be best put into play and understood. Without an understanding of the purpose of collaboration, the outcomes never create the most wins for everyone.

Groupthink Relies on Consensus

Collaboration is more than decision by committee, where people come to an agreement rather than focusing on the best solution. In a committee decision, people tend to want to come to a consensus. They often put their best ideas aside and give in to whatever most of the room wants to do. This is also groupthink.

When collaboration is at work, people present their ideas even when they know they aren't popular ideas. They express their opinions even when they're not aligned with the opinions of the loudest people in the room. Individuals who know how to collaborate fight for their voices to be heard, knowing that the group understands the value of their voice and will consider it in the solution.

People whose minds go straight to "decision by committee" don't speak up, and they don't always listen to those who do. They are eager to reach a consensus, the minimum requirement to get a project done.

Groupthink Involves a Division of Labor

The main roadblock to successful collaboration occurs when the division of labor is mistaken for collaboration. This misconception is rooted in the belief that splitting the work among individuals is the same as collaboration and results in more getting done in less time. However, involving too many people in a project can actually slow down the process.

This isn't factory work where everyone stands at an assembly line and puts in a little bit of effort—it's knowledge work. The problems that collaboration solve don't require manual labor, and so a simple division of labor is not the solution. If the work can simply be broken apart and delegated without examining the core of the issue, it's not collaborative. That's a joint effort.

True collaboration is necessitated by not knowing how to solve a problem. In collaboration, more people, perspectives, and ideas come together to go beyond solving the problem to backing up and trying to look at it in the right way. The goal is not to complete a project as quickly as possible, but to capitalize on the skills of the right individuals to create a balance of maximum wins within an acceptable timeline. Collaboration is acknowledging that with the right perspectives, you can solve something much bigger. Even if it's not the fastest solution, it's the right solution.

Working to find the right solutions makes the time spent less relevant. Who cares how long the win took as long as you got the outcome you needed rather than cutting corners and coming up short? Collaboration is about achieving more in terms of quality than quantity by finding a more sustainable, equitable, and informed solution.

Putting more people on an assembly line might be the fastest way to make a car, but it doesn't mean the car is better. Inefficient collaboration affects qualitative results everywhere. If a team is burned out and exhausted from one collaborative project gone wrong, productivity stalls elsewhere. But, if people go into collaboration with a clear understanding of what they want to achieve together, the win affects everyone. The collaborators come away satisfied and more ready and willing to take on the next collaboration.

A CLOSER LOOK:
THE COMMITTEE CATASTROPHE

Have you ever been on a committee where no one could agree on the best solution, so everyone agreed on a lukewarm one just so that they could just finish the project and go home? You come away knowing you've found a solution, but you don't feel good about it. You could have done better.

I'm sure you have. Today's workplace is chock full of situations like this.

Take Diversity and Inclusion committees, for example. Sherri might volunteer because she's not already on a committee or Jonathan might be forced to volunteer by higher ups, but they're both white and so they may not have a personal stake in the conversation. That doesn't mean that they shouldn't be there or even that they shouldn't lead the conversation, but if they're brought together without considering their strengths and values as individual players, they aren't set up to collaborate.

Everyone in the group, Sherri and Jonathan included, should have something to gain and lose in the conversation. They should be invested in creating wins for everyone, including those who aren't in the room. If someone has a stake in the outcome but isn't part of the conversation, they should invite them in. They should all have the gravitas to share their ideas, even if they started at the company four days ago and aren't sure how their ideas will be received.

Think of the last time you participated in or witnessed a committee catastrophe. How could the group have collaborated, and how might that have resulted in more wins?

COLLABORATING STRATEGICALLY AND INTENTIONALLY

Collaboration requires more than sharing the workload or getting more people involved in a committee. It demands a new approach that benefits everyone.

A new approach begins with a different mindset. The star player or the smartest kid in the group has to believe that instead of having much to lose, they have much to gain; they can come out a winner, and *all* the players, whatever their contribution, can come out winners too. Strategic, intentional collaboration—done with purpose and accountability—achieves more for everyone, uncovering better solutions and delivering more wins.

In this chapter, we have explored some of the main reasons collaborations fail, but I have saved the big one for last, and have dedicated the following chapter to it. It's a fundamental misconception of what collaboration is. I call it "The Kumbaya Effect."

4

THE KUMBAYA EFFECT

13 minute read

THERE IS A DISEASE SPREADING LIKE WILDFIRE IN MEETING rooms, on team projects, and throughout companies everywhere. This aberration imitates, and is often mistaken for, collaboration. The name of this imposter is... the *Kumbaya Effect*.

Early symptoms of the Kumbaya Effect include being part of a team project or pseudo-collaboration with friendly meetings that go nowhere. Symptoms worsen over time, as follows:

- The inability to distinguish between one of those meetings and an awkward dinner party

- Feelings of camaraderie and activity but no progress or productivity

- A reluctance to voice an opinion or disagree with an opinion

- Short spurts of cheer and hopefulness that quickly turn to frustration and hopelessness

- Sadness brought on by settling for mediocrity

- An overwhelming sense of impending doom

- Stress, constipation, bloating, and nausea

The prognosis of the Kumbaya Effect is a slow and painful death to innovation, creativity, motivation, and big wins.

If you or a loved one have experienced the Kumbaya Effect, don't despair—there is a cure. This chapter serves as your complimentary prescription for a single dose of anti-Kumbaya, administered by yours truly. Keep reading—and start treatment immediately!

THE CAUSES

Nobody calls a Kumbaya Meeting or puts a Kumbaya Project on their schedule. If they did, it would be called the company picnic or the holiday party.

Kumbaya meetings and projects are not actual work, and we shouldn't pretend that they are. They're definitely not collaboration. Yet we often get pulled into these get-togethers, where a problem is sort of discussed and a solution is sort of reached, but the primary goal seems to be "don't ruffle any feathers and let's all try to get out of here alive."

If the Kumbaya Effect is so nonproductive, why does it exist? Where did it come from and why does it persist?

External Forces at Work

The Kumbaya Effect can be the result of externally imposed demands to collaborate. Remember my son's group project? He was expected to collaborate when he would have preferred to complete the project on his own. Not that he's collaboration-averse, but he knew that with no guidelines or accountability, it was destined to fail, or at least cause him a lot of stress.

My son had no input on the team members or their skills. His teacher just lumped a certain number of people into each group and expected them to work it out and provide a completed project of a certain length on a certain topic within a certain amount of time. There is some glorification of "working together" at play here. That sounds kind of crazy until you consider how many team projects you've been tasked with that have played out exactly the same way.

It's no surprise that we don't revolt. After all, externally imposed "togetherness" trained us to accept externally imposed *work* projects. And to sit down, shut up, and join in on the next chorus of *Kumbaya*.

Careers aren't middle school, no matter how much we like our coworkers. And sitting around the campfire roasting marshmallows does not produce big wins for anybody. The Kumbaya Effect doesn't translate when the end goal is not just some elusive good feeling. When you're really trying to get something done, there has to be different ground rules.

Confusing Camaraderie for Collaboration

Even people who haven't had nightmarish team project experiences often avoid collaboration. They see it as a lot of unproductive time spent with coworkers, delivering mediocre outcomes.

Sure, everyone got along. There were no truly awful feelings or major conflicts. No one carried most of the load, and no one slacked off. Everyone did enough work to get the job done. In fact, the whole experience was extremely easy—so much fun, you wanted to gather everyone around the campfire, break out the marshmallows (or the weenies, depending on your charred food preferences), and sing *Kumbaya*.

But deep down, you knew something was wrong. Despite all the touchy-feely goodness of working together toward a shared goal, the end result was as stale and mediocre as a day-old s'more. You could have aimed higher. You could have done better. You could have done *more*.

There's nothing wrong with connecting with colleagues on a personal level, but don't mistake connection for collaboration. It is merely a placebo that replaces the awesomeness of big wins with the pleasantness of camaraderie.

Experiences like these make people collaboration-phobic. They see collaboration as an altruistic endeavor that's little more than an exercise in futility, as far as doing their best work goes. The return on their time and effort is minimal, and with both at a premium, they don't see these exercises as worth their while.

THE EFFECTS

Beyond the obvious negative impacts of the Kumbaya Effect, other more subtle effects infiltrate. In a way, these effects poison the productivity and the innovation that businesses in today's competitive growth-focused businesses crave.

Guilt over Self-Interest

One result of the Kumbaya Effect is feelings of guilt for wanting more for yourself.

Everyone should want something for themselves, and there is no shame in self-interest. It's how we survive as communities, industries, companies, and individuals. But people are often made to feel that if they don't want to participate in the Kumbaya, they are not a team player.

If teamwork and collaboration feel icky to you, you're not alone. If they make you feel like you're settling but you're afraid to ask for more, you are not alone. Seeking a bigger, better outcome for your time and effort and wanting more for yourself isn't selfish. You *can* get what you want and create more wins for everyone.

Collaboration is not an altruistic fantasy, so why do so many people see it that way? Possibly because that is the acceptable way to couch it. But what if we were able to ask for collaboration out of self interest, coupled with an interest for other things as well?

People get it wrong from the start. They set up team projects as a façade of collaboration, when their real goal is the perceived emotional gain from working together—the Kumbaya Effect. When people misinterpret collaboration as simply working in proximity, the whole purpose of collaboration is derailed.

Again, camaraderie is not collaboration. Standing at the bus stop together doesn't mean you're all going to the same place. You might sit on the same bench, get on the same bus, and even sit next to each other, but you no doubt have your eyes on different stops.

Both camaraderie and collaboration bring people together, but that's where the similarities end. With camaraderie, random people are invited to contribute their presence and skills in the hope that something wonderful will happen. With collaboration, people are intentionally chosen for their skills and are expected to contribute to a shared end goal. They are supposed to seek out the best solution with the most wins.

They will not always agree. Their Kumbaya may get woefully offbeat and out of tune at times. That's what happens when thinking people come together with their best ideas. People who, at times, are willing to fight for those ideas in their own self-interests, while perhaps considering the interests of others (but always with something in it for themselves).

Shifting your thinking about collaborative projects means putting away the marshmallows, backing away from the campfire, and setting yourself up for collaborative success.

One-sided Relationships

Another negative impact of the Kumbaya Effect is that it creates or coalesces a relationship structure that is one-sided.

Say you have a business downtown and someone approaches you to join a downtown alliance. They're not asking whether you have a vested interest in the nonprofit, whether you have anything to gain or lose by serving on their committee; they're not asking you for your input on possible solutions; they're just asking for you to join, and your sponsorship is expected largely because you're in proximity. This happens with many community efforts.

Since businesses profit, they should give it away, right? We've created a world where we expect billionaires to solve world hunger, and make it socially acceptable to shame them into giving their money away. This is the Kumbaya Effect in action. It's easier to go around the fire ring and find someone else who should fix things without the work of an intentional plan of collaboration between all of the different organizations and players. But the truth is that without mindful collaboration, even if they gave all the money, it won't meet the heart of the need and create the most wins possible.

The Kumbaya Effect is all about how many people you gather around the campfire, but true collaboration considers *who* you gather together and what is expected of them and given to them in exchange. Newsflash—the size of your fire ring doesn't matter.

If a business owner wants something out of a partnership with a nonprofit, they may think it's impossible for them to work together, but that isn't the case. There's nothing wrong with wanting something in return. We can't work for free, not because people aren't lovely like that but because structurally it is not sustainable.

In fact, this give-and-receive model is already cemented through tax breaks. Tax breaks help advance both the giver and the receiver's goals, which benefits the community at large. However, we can create much bigger wins than tax breaks, especially because tax breaks don't always apply to all forms of generosity.

For example, if a company builds a free website for a nonprofit, they don't get a tax break because they paid their own employees to build it. There's no write-off for giving away time and expertise, so what's the incentive for the employees working harder? Maybe it's something like this: the nonprofit could promote the business in return by featuring the company's logo on the website. Putting the company out there gets more opportunities for work, which increases employees' wages and gives everyone the ability to be more generous. If businesses were invited to be open about their best interest and unashamedly get "something out of it," beyond the invisible trophy of altruism, a better conversation could emerge.

Don't be shy about wanting something for your company because wanting a win for your company is the same as wanting a win for your people. Additionally, promoting your charitable contributions is especially important in a tight labor market when you're trying to attract and retain the best and brightest talent who want to work for a company that lets them be a part of something bigger.

Like we've talked about before, everyone has agendas and that's okay—as long as they're open about it. It's impossible for people to come together and not have goals of their own. You can help others, but you have to take care of yourself, too. When we go beyond transactional one-sided giving, we can create a collaboration that multiplies wins exponentially.

BEYOND KUMBAYA

Collaboration isn't the same thing as camaraderie or Kumbaya, but it isn't evil either. If anything, it's a more honest approach to doing a job well for yourself and for others. Some might say that's selfish, especially the "for yourself" part, but isn't everything we do beneficial to ourselves in some way?

In other words, is there really such a thing as altruism? Not really. Good acts, even when done anonymously, offer something to the person who performs them. The payoff might be internal—feeling good about making a donation, for example. Or, it could be external, such as receiving a tax break for making the donation. No matter how noble an agenda, it's still an agenda. We shouldn't attack each other for advancing our own agendas or for not supporting someone else's if it doesn't work with ours. Collaboration allows us to work together to advance our agendas together *while* expanding the wins for others.

This kind of thinking works with our very human need to advance our own agendas. What defines the core of humanity more than that? If it weren't for the people who weren't afraid to want more, we'd never have advances in technology or medicine. Assuming that advancing one's own agenda is wrong and seeking to build systems that advance only one person's agenda are losing propositions. There should be no shame in doing better for oneself—and this is especially true when you can help others in the process.

When the goal of "collaboration" is an ephemeral good feeling, everyone is focused on compromising their ideas to appease everyone else and maintain the feel-good Kumbaya, rather than finding the best solution that invites innovation and meets needs. To combat the Kumbaya Effect, we need targeted, intentional collaboration. We're adults, and we should be choosing who we're sitting around the campfire with and what songs we sing.

I'm not suggesting we throw camaraderie out the window and prepare for battle. Getting along and playing nice with others has a place in collaboration. Just be aware of it, prepare for it, and don't let it take over. It is not the primary objective.

Set an Agenda

The easiest way to prevent connection, camaraderie, and personal discussions from derailing productivity in collaborative talks is to put it right there on the agenda. Designate the first few minutes of the meeting as time for everyone to get to know each other or catch up since the last time they met. Depending on the number of people and the time available, this could take five to twenty minutes or longer.

Giving people that time allows them to get it all out of their system so they can focus on the primary agenda item—whatever problem you're trying to solve or goal you're trying to meet. It also serves the helpful purpose of camaraderie—connecting people on a personal level so they'll work better together. Then, you can get on with the real matter at hand with clarity, focus, and collaboration.

If you're struggling to break free from the Kumbaya Effect, use this meeting questionnaire before, during, and after your meeting to stay on track with collaboration and prevent Kumbaya from derailing your intention and solutions.

Before the meeting:

- What is the purpose of us working together?

- What intended outcome is the meeting agenda supporting?

- Do we have a set time for personal connection in the agenda?

- How can we match our objectives to the choice of people we are intentionally bringing together?

During the meeting:

- Start with a designated time for connection.

- Identify the strength everyone brings to the table and in what way each person is contributing to the objectives.

- What do you have to gain or lose?

- What hidden agendas does everyone have?

- In what ways can we create bigger wins?

After the meeting:

- Were there any ideas that you didn't share or felt like you couldn't contribute?

- Is the workload and individual input properly distributed?

- Is one person exerting undue influence?

- What is the cost/benefit analysis of time and energy exerted during the group meeting versus individual effort?

- What solution did you find, and was it the best solution or the most common denominator?

- Of the wins you created as a group, which ones were unexpected?

- How are the group wins bigger than possible individual wins?

A CLOSER LOOK: BEIMDIEK

When collaborating for the benefit of the community at large, imaginative thinking is just as important as who you invite into the room.

I was asked by Beimdiek, now Assured Partners, an insurance company, to talk to them about increasing their social media presence. When I met with Steve Beimdiek, the company president, I told him, "I appreciate that you've invited me in, but I can make this meeting short for you. You can make a Facebook account to advertise your business, but you shouldn't because people won't be interested in following it. Most people find insurance boring. That's my opinion, and I can leave—or we can stop thinking about this relationship as transactional and instead use this time to think about something bigger."

Steve let me stay and change the conversation, so I asked him to tell me what their company cares about, which is how I learned about Beimdiek's generosity toward the community. They loved donating to the community, but they didn't want to toot their own horn—but why? I asked Steve to consider how it would be a big win for his employees to be aware of how much the company was giving back to the community. Also, I wondered if he could see the importance of educating people about how significant local support is to so many amazing organizations.

As we talked, we also realized that we could promote their generosity and others' externally by making a social media account focused on recognizing those who give back. We used Facebook to launch what we called the Beimdiek Mega Fan Dome, named because Beimdiek was a mega fan of all of the amazing things that people do in the community.

As the owner of a marketing agency, I'm frequently asked to sponsor charity events in my town. Because of this experience, I know that nonprofits often need tents for events that cost hundreds, if not thousands, of dollars to rent, so I suggested that Beimdiek buy one of those tents and loan it to charities for free. Now every time there's a community event, the Beimdiek tent is set up free of charge. Of course, I designed an amazing graphic for Beimdiek, so the company gets brand recognition and serves the community at the same time. Everyone's a winner: the company, the nonprofits, the community, the employees, and the people the charities serve.

Since starting to loan the Beimdiek tent, the company has given out labeled water at races, bought a company-branded truck to transport the tent, bought TV spots to feature charities, and hosted a yearly nonprofit grant. They also realized that nonprofits not only need donations but also exposure. A large company like Beimdiek could give them the exposure that raised their visibility and helped bring in donations from other companies and individuals.

All of the giving didn't need to come out of their pocket. Beimdiek used the marketing money they were already spending to collaborate with nonprofits and highlight those organizations—while also expanding their own company's exposure. The Beimdiek Mega Fan Dome was much bigger than the transactional thinking of just writing a check. We found opportunities for them to truly collaborate for bigger, bolder wins for more people.

Some people believe it's more genuinely altruistic to quietly donate money; I see it as a wasted opportunity to create a bigger win. When you get hooked into the Kumbaya Effect, you miss the chance to expand your impact. Few companies are willing to use their imaginations and think bigger, beyond themselves, but once they understand how to take advantage of their platform, they can create huge wins for more people.

LEAVE KUMBAYA FOR THE CAMPFIRE

People are often hesitant to collaborate because it's been misrepresented as a summer camp Kumbaya experience. Nebulous feelings of togetherness don't amount to real change. Collaboration is coming together to find the right solution that you couldn't have gained on an individual level. If you're not sharing your hidden agendas and acknowledging that everyone can win, you'll never find the best solution that benefits everyone.

Stop forcing people to gather in kumbaya circles and work around each other's hidden agendas for the perceived benefit of a feel-good experience. Instead, let's bring people together in a meaningful way for an intentional purpose with specific goals and awareness of what each person has to contribute.

Don't stop at asking whether you got something done. The real question is, was it the right thing? There's not a point to collaboration for the sake of collaboration. If you don't know why you're working together, or are working together because it will be different, you're not reaching your goals. You don't care to do it differently—you want to do it right.

5

WHY COLLABORATION IS THE NEW COMPETITION

11 minute read

IT'S TIME TO LET GO OF THE FAILED COLLABORATIONS THAT derailed your success in fifth grade group projects and ruined your attitude toward team projects at work. We're not going to hold hands and sing folk songs. We *are* going to figure out how to do collaboration the right way. Shift your mindset and be open to the possibilities of what can be achieved with a different approach.

"But Priscilla," I hear you saying, "do I really have to rethink EVERYTHING?"

Yes. Yes you do.

Why? Because the world market is not a field of dreams, and "If you build it, they will come" doesn't play out the way it used to. In the digital age, everyone, every company, is a drop in a bucket. Or to stick with the theme, an ear of corn in a field as big as Nebraska. The only way to stay relevant is to be aware of what's happening around you and find opportunities for collaboration.

Technological progress moves at an incredibly fast pace, driving disruption in all industries. Brand loyalty is a thing of the past, and no company can rely on the same customer base to continue buying their products and services. Today's consumers are loyal to their own in-the-moment values, convenience, and concerns. Companies can't survive just by being the biggest player on the block anymore. The global market has invited many more players to the game. In today's fast-paced, ultra-saturated digital age, collaboration is the only way to survive, let alone compete.

You're not just competing with someone who lives down the street, but with everyone around the globe. Consumers are going out into the global economy for all of their purchases, even if what they're looking for is available in their neighborhood. If you think that a consumer is going to find you out of billions of options, here's some context: there are 1.8 billion websites in the world. Yes, you read that right: billion with a *b*. With nearly two billion websites to choose from, and only a handful that immediately pop up on a search page, how will you capture a consumer's attention? You can be a very large company and drive that discoverability yourself (say, with SEO and other tools), or you can start collaborating more effectively.

Large companies handle the modern hurdle to discoverability by creating huge digital ad spreads and landing a commercial in the Superbowl. For everyone else who doesn't have a seven-figure marketing budget, collaborating more effectively is the only way to get noticed. Smaller businesses can set out on their own and be overlooked, or they can realize that in order to compete, they need to utilize active and effective collaboration.

Individuals can solve their own problems, but often at a price: it takes longer, costs more, and demands more effort than collaboration. Say there are five people trying to solve a problem. Three of them collaborate, share resources, and solve the problem. The other two solve it only for themselves. Whose solution is going to have the greatest insight? Which solution is more likely to disrupt the industry? (Here's a hint: not the people who are navel-gazing.)

YOU HAVE TO CONNECT

Collaboration begins with connecting. Look for commonalities between problems that everyone is trying to solve and identify solutions that you can share.

You Are Already Connecting *and* Collaborating

If you aren't sure where to start, the good news is that most of us are already collaborating without realizing it. For your company to have survived this far, you more than likely have a digital presence. The foundation of social media is built on collaboration.

Take LinkedIn, a platform that most business professionals use. Every day, there are sixty-one million senior-level influencers and sixty-five million decision makers on LinkedIn.[4] Without even realizing it, job-seekers and established professionals are already collaborating in order to compete. Job-seekers don't get out the yellow pages and call businesses, asking if they have any open positions. A job opens up, and candidates are noticed because they have a LinkedIn profile

---

4 https://www.google.com/url?q=https://news.linkedin.com/about-us%23Statistics&sa=D&source=docs&ust=1681136717047622&usg=AOvVaw2nPcoCHm-D6eOOAiQup06SR

and a network of connections that brings attention to their qualifications. A message later, and they have an interview.

That's collaboration, even if it seems subtle. The candidate is collaborating with LinkedIn, a company that receives platform activity in exchange for its users creating profiles. In order to compete, candidates leverage a larger space and the relationships they have with people at other companies. Because individuals take so much initiative on platforms like LinkedIn, companies must replicate this chain of interaction on a bigger scale to become and remain relevant to buyers.

You Can Connect Earlier

The modern buyer's journey is largely self-directed and anonymous.

The first thing people do when they need something is use what I call their "Google thumbs." They may go into a casual or a formal research mode, but regardless of the rigor, they are doing this anonymously. In fact, Gartner research found that when B2B buyers are considering a purchase, they spend only 17% of that time meeting with potential suppliers."[5] This

---

5   https://www.gartner.com/en/sales/insights/b2b-buying-journey

leaves 83% of the buyer's journey out of the purview of the sales professional.

People don't want to be sold to—they want to find solutions to their own problems. They do their own reconnaissance. They conduct their own due diligence. The buyer can access so much information on their own that they can make their own decisions without salespeople, and make them quickly. In fact, according to a study from FocusVision, now Forsta, the average B2B buyer's journey involves consumption of 13 pieces of content before making a buying decision.[6]

Louder sales pitches won't break through buyers' self-direction. Market research shows that consumers won't tolerate overt sales and impersonal messages that inundate them until they break. No one volunteers to spend their weekend at a used car dealership because they love sales pitches.

Additionally, a brand name isn't as influential as it once was. In the face of waning brand loyalty, thought leadership seems to be operating as a type of proxy. In fact, according to Edelman-LinkedIn Research, 58% of B2B decision makers said they chose a business based on their thought leadership.[7]

---

6 https://martech.org/b2b-buyers-consume-an-average-of-13-content-pieces-before-deciding-on-a-vendor/

7 https://www.socialmediatoday.com/news/study-b2b-marketers-underestimate-the-power-of-thought-leadership/554499/

Brand isn't as important as knowing if the company's representatives are best in class and can solve the challenges they have due to their command of their area of expertise. The powerful implication here is that well-positioned and more socially influential companies can use thought leadership and micro-influencer tactics to gain a larger share of their target market's attention.

Given this data, the most pressing concerns for companies are how to insert themselves earlier in the buyer journey; how to be seen as the expert; and how to ensure that many of the thirteen pieces of content buyers read are authored by them.

You Can Turn Passive Collaboration into Active Collaboration

One of the easiest ways to leverage your current connections is by turning passive collaboration into active collaboration. Simply having a LinkedIn profile is passive collaboration; using it to engage with others is active collaboration, which gives you a competitive advantage over others in the same space who remain passive.

When it comes to networks, the more effort you put in, the more you get in return. For example, you're already collaborating by having a LinkedIn profile, but what if you were to actively engage with your network?

There are 900 million members on LinkedIn,[8] but a personal network will never grow to that number of individuals. Make a conscious effort to narrow your focus to only your current and most ideal potential customers. The moment you try to be everything to everybody is the moment that you become nothing to everyone. Instead, fine-tune your messages and interactions to set the stage for collaboration. Find other thought leaders in your space, combine your specialties, and collaborate in a way that expands each of your audiences.

But to do this well, you need to know who in your professional network might make a good collaborator and what you have to share.

Ask yourself basically the same question, but from multiple angles using this Collaboration Prep Sheet:[9]

- Whom do I serve?

- What are recurring questions or themes my most ideal client is struggling with?

- How do I uniquely solve problems?

---

8 https://www.google.com/url?q=https://about.linkedin.com/&sa=D&source=do cs&ust=1681136716964420&usg=AOvVaw0DB7TaNlTB_WCSk-owQTfH

9 All free downloads created for this book can be found at priscillamckinney.com/ collaboration-downloads

- What are some of my best and brightest thoughts that have made a difference in the past?

- How can I build rapport and get known for what I do?

- How do I couch the sharing of my thought leadership and expertise?

- How can I be seen as a problem solver?

- How can I speak the same language the customer uses in their buyer's journey and let go of industry jargon to explain things?

Once you've asked yourself these questions, it's time to consider something totally new—collaborating with your competitors.

Collaborating with Competitors

Competitive collaboration is about asking how to expand your audience without having to create it yourself. Look for the intersection of needs and what you have to win and lose. Instead of trying to indirectly appeal to your audience on your own, collaborate with someone who has a common target audience and expand both of your platforms.

For example, I often feature authors who are experts in a certain field on my podcast, Ponderings from the Perch.[10] By being featured, they gain access to the ten thousand listeners of my show, and their followers are incentivized to listen to my podcast. We both win, and the listener wins too.

Before these interviews, I ask what they would like to get out of the interview. Then toward the end of our recording time, I tee them up so they never have to sound salesy. It's my way of thanking them for their time and actively collaborating for a bigger win beyond the episode.

However, collaboration isn't just about finding people who have a bigger audience. You want to actively collaborate with people who make sense for your ideal client. Additionally, both parties need to have something to offer. Otherwise, one person will be doing all the work while the other reaps all the benefits.

For example, my friend Andy Crestodina, founder of Orbit Media Studios and author of *Content Chemistry,* is recognized as a thought leader within the marketing space because he has his finger on the pulse of the industry's concerns and direction. He does this by constantly connecting and collaborating online with his colleagues, as well as constantly sharing his expertise. I never host my company's annual Insights Marketing Day without asking Andy to speak.

---

10 https://podcast.littlebirdmarketing.com

Every year, Andy does a massive survey within marketing. In 2022, he shared "New Blogging Statistics: What Content Strategies Work in 2022? We asked 1016 Bloggers," an article that included "26 charts based on those responses, input from the top industry experts and a set of blogging statistics that reveal some fascinating insights into an industry in flux, now more than ever." But he doesn't share others' ideas without crediting them; throughout the article, he quotes his collaborators, establishing them as thought leaders among his own audience.

Andy understands the power of leveraging collaboration, along with thought leadership and micro-influencing tactics, to create wins for everyone. This increases their reach and gets their name on a bigger stage.

Andy Crestodina and I shouldn't be friends based on traditional business rules. We're in the same industry, so our target audiences are the same, and Andy already has a major following. We could be competing for clients, but instead we leverage each other's platforms so that we both win. When I feature him on my podcast, he shares it on social media. As a result, more people discover my podcast, which generates more subscribers. On my end, I have regular listeners who discover his platform and want to engage with him further.

I often collaborate with my two major competitors to leverage our influence and create bigger wins because we all understand that we're bigger together than we are individually. I'm not worried that my competitors are also reaching more clients because it's about quality of interaction over quantity. We all draw more clients who then get to choose the company that is the best fit for their needs. Through collaboration, we are each able to better connect with our ideal clients and focus on our specialties, rather than wasting that energy competing with each other.

A CLOSER LOOK: INSIGHTS MARKETING DAY

Insight Marketing Day, a major collaboration among competing marketing businesses, was originally hosted by Green-Book, an association that serves insight professionals. When they decided they no longer had the bandwidth for the event, they looked to two companies that they had previously hosted, including mine, Little Bird Marketing.

Both of our companies had leaders who had spoken at the events, and the companies "played nicely together." Green-Book asked if we would be open to collaborating together to keep the important event going. Our companies would pay for it, but GreenBook would lend us the Insight Marketing Day name, allowing us to leverage the history and the brand while maintaining the credibility that it had earned over the years. GreenBook's win was the ability to continue offering the event to their audience, and the companies that took it over won with the exposure and influence gained through the event.

The other business, which was one of our direct competitors, is located in the UK, and we've divided responsibilities equally. When the event is hosted in the UK, I am a speaker, and when we host in America, we have a slot for one of their speakers.

Even though we create bigger wins through our collaboration, there is still something to lose in terms of reputation. We don't share our IP or trade secrets (since we're competing as separate entities), but because we're working in such close proximity, they're going to know more than our other competitors, such as if my business is in trouble, if we're doing well, or if an employee has left. We have something to lose by getting closer, but we also have something very strong to gain as well. Because we have established trust by creating a framework and ground rules, our collaboration is immensely successful for everyone involved.

Before we go into more detail about how to collaborate, consider how you can make the most out of your network:

- List all of the online platforms you're a part of. How do you interact now? In what ways could you create more meaningful interactions that could result in collaboration?

- Are you a member of any associations or organizations? How can you leverage this network and be more actively involved?

- What collaborations do you already have? What are some opportunities to expand those relationships?

- Create a plan for regular interactions, even if it's spending just fifteen minutes on LinkedIn at the start of every day.

We can't do business as usual anymore. We have to be dynamic in response to a dynamic world. Doing the bare minimum and hoping that it's all going to work out is the same as digging a grave for your company.

DIGITAL, TARGETED COLLABORATION

The over-saturation of our digital age means that acting on our own isn't enough. I'll say that a different way—acting together and not alone is no longer a nicety; it's a necessity.

My company's entire network used to fit in a Rolodex on my desk. We could only keep up with dozens of relationships, and the frequency of touch was weekly or monthly. The trust people had with us was anecdotal, and we struggled to stay top-of-mind.

Now that technology has made connectivity easy and immediate, our network has expanded exponentially. We are constantly interacting with our network through social media. The frequency of touch is real-time: people knew when I moved my office and when my daughter graduated. They knew when I had surgery and when we won big accounts. Trust becomes proven because there is social proof for recommendations, testimonials, work experience, and awards—all easily accessible.

Unseen is unsold. When more people see your company, they recognize you as experts, which increases your influence *and* your sales—and effective collaboration provides greater visibility. You just have to understand the framework and ground rules before you jump into your next collaboration.

6

THE FRAMEWORK AND GROUND RULES

11 minute read

NOW THAT WE'VE COVERED HOW TO USE COLLABORATION competitively, it's time to give you the seven easy steps of collaboration!

Just joking. As I said earlier, there are none.

Complex problems are just that: complex. After all, collaboration is about connecting as people, and we know that humans are anything but straightforward. When you dive into different ideas, communication styles, and agendas, collaboration can get messy. No rigid structure will result in successful collaboration because collaboration is different each time. For collaboration to work, you need to change your approach to fit every situation.

Consider a problem you currently have and imagine what it would look like when it's done. Now imagine what it looks like when it's done well. Isn't that better? Well, you won't get there with a cookie-cutter solution. It takes imagination. It takes innovation.

That doesn't mean guard rails don't exist. There has to be some kind of strategy to create the desired outcome of your collaboration. To collaborate in order to compete, you need a framework that empowers people, teams, and communities to think more expansively. Following a framework and agreeing to basic ground rules creates collaboration that will give you the competitive advantage you need to get ahead and stay ahead.

A conceptual framework allows for innovation and creativity that meets the issue at its core instead of developing surface-level solutions. The right framework guides the building of something expansive, whereas prescriptive steps limit, preclude, and minimize.

Why do we need a framework? Well, humans are conceptual by nature. We use patterns or structures to function logically and make sense of our world. But, when conceptual structure becomes rigid and rote, it doesn't support the building of something bigger— the creative, dynamic solution that creates the most wins for everyone.

Cookie-cutter structures create cookie-cutter solutions. We can do better than that.

BUILDING THE FRAMEWORK

You need some type of structure, but it doesn't have to be prescriptive. Complex issues can't be limited to a linear progression when the solution requires expansive, fluid thinking. People who follow steps might be doing all the "right" things, but they could easily do them in the wrong order. And when they get so focused on putting one foot in front of the other, they can't see the obstacles in front of them. They also can't see beyond the path, so they miss opportunities.

Working within a framework, on the other hand, amplifies possibilities within a safe structure. The structure acts like a flashlight that prevents you from stumbling around in the dark of collaboration, but it doesn't limit your progress.

To understand what framework will be the most helpful, we need to consider the people we need, how everyone will be held accountable, and what type of thinking the problem requires.

Get the Right People at the Table

Throwing a bunch of random people in a room and asking them to solve a problem might work for escape rooms, but it isn't the best way to collaborate. You'll have a better outcome if you invite the *right* people into that room (this also works for escape rooms, by the way).

How do you select the right people? Instead of starting with a checklist of surface-level characteristics, dictated largely by each individual's company title, think more deeply. Do you need a CEO in the room? Or would the executive assistant be a better choice for your particular problem?

To get started, look for parity and equity.

Seek Parity

Parity means looking at the equal representation of values that people have to offer beyond their title, salary, or social status. When you think about parity, you need to think like a social scientist. Consider the possible interactions between everyone based on multiple levels.

For example, if I'm working out a problem for an art foundation, imagine that I have a fifty-year-old billionaire CEO and a twenty-five-year-old receptionist at the table. Despite their differences, in this example, both the CEO and receptionist have perspectives that are valuable, and I need input from them equally. I need to know what kind of event the billionaire art collector wants to attend and support, and I also need the receptionist's perspective, because he has experience mobilizing volunteers at art organizations and charity events.

How do you create parity so that the receptionist doesn't keep his mouth shut while the CEO dominates the conversation? This is where having ground rules can help make sure everyone has an equal stake in the game and is fully contributing to the success of the collaboration.

Seek Equity

To me, equity isn't about balancing gender or race. It's about balancing stakeholders' voices and getting a true representation of the issue.

It's necessary to hear from everyone who will be affected by the collaboration, but that doesn't necessarily mean that every person will have the same level of involvement in the collaboration. Collaboration becomes unwieldy when there are too many perspectives in the mix who are also decision makers. However, those who aren't actively contributing can still be called on for their input and consultation. A consideration of equity creates a boundary between listening to everyone's perspective and those who are responsible for action and the overall outcome.

For true equity, everyone must have something to lose and something to gain. These potential wins and losses don't have to be fair or equal in value, but equitable in that the concept applies to all parties.

In the example above, the CEO would want to gain prestige through association with the art foundation, but she is also donating money. The receptionist is a new dad and his time is in just as much demand as the CEO's, but he also cares deeply about the art community and is passionate about supporting the foundation.

Ask yourself: *Who will this collaboration impact, and are they represented here in this collaboration? What do the people in this room stand to lose and to gain?*

Foster a Range of Leadership Styles

With more people involved, there must be a governing body. It takes a lot to manage human beings, and there needs to be someone at the helm who knows how to lead collaboration; who can organize where, when, and how you'll collaborate; and who creates a sense of accountability.

Since no two collaborations are the same, different styles of leadership are needed for different problems. Consider if there is a particular type of leader who will work best in your situation. Do you need someone to handle more of the administrative and organizational tasks, such as deciding when and where to meet, what the next steps are, and how you'll communicate? Or do you need someone who keeps the group in touch with the empathy of the issue and who knows how to listen, create space for people and ideas, and prevent groupthink?

Whatever style of leadership is chosen, it needs to be conducive to ongoing collaboration.

Create Accountability

To ensure that your collaboration doesn't remind anyone of fifth-grade class projects gone wrong, you need to ensure your leaders establish a system of accountability. When each member understands their responsibilities and the consequences of stalling progress, the collaboration will successfully reach the best solutions.

Accountability could look like a gamified tally of numbers and contributions of each member. Or, it could be constant check-ins, hard deadlines, required progress before each meeting, and a checklist that shows what actions need to be completed and who is responsible for each. Maybe a third party, such as a project management board, is created to oversee the collaboration and hold everyone accountable.

Ask yourself: *What are the repercussions for not getting something done, and who will keep track of everyone's contributions and deadlines?*

Allow Critical Thinking

Collaboration requires critical thinking and creative approaches to problem solving. Sometimes this means going against what's common or what's popular.

For example, leaning in isn't always the answer. In some situations, maybe you should not only lean out, but run the other way. Maybe you should vote with your lack of presence and avoid complicity in systems and organizations that aren't in alignment with your values.

I once collaborated with a colleague to create a clubhouse networking event for our industry. As soon as we started sharing ideas, it was clear that our visions didn't align. I wanted to create a fun environment for casual conversations, whereas he wanted to facilitate serious discussion about hard-hitting subjects. Because we went through the steps of creating a framework and strategy, we realized that our collaboration wasn't going to work. We are still friends and trusted colleagues because the failure or success of the clubhouse wasn't the goal. We kept collaborating—just not on that project.

Thinking critically ensures that you have awareness about how and why you're collaborating. There are times to collaborate and other times when you shouldn't, which is another reason to do it strategically and purposefully.

Consider, do you know when collaboration isn't working and when to quit? If not, you're not collaborating. You're participating in a committee.

GROUND RULES

Once you have the framework, then you need to have some ground rules for how everyone participates. Ground rules help to increase the likelihood of success because they tie into the concept of accountability. Unless you agree on ground rules, define your expectations, and document them, they are not actionable.

For instance, I was once on the board of a women's committee that put on a yearly gala at our town's art museum. Since the goal of the gala was to raise money, we did a lot of the setup and technical work ourselves. Our committee had a ground rule that on the night of the gala, after all of the guests were gone, everyone was required to swap out their gown for sweats and help clean up the venue. If you didn't want to clean, you had to write a large donation check to be excused. (You can imagine I was more than happy to change and help clean.) This ground rule was a creative way to set the expectation of equal participation and that there were consequences for unequal contributions.

After more collaborations than I can count (or even remember), I've developed a list of ground rules that work in most instances.

No sharing of IP or company secrets. Even though you're creating bigger wins together, be aware that your collaborator may still be your competitor. Set ground rules to create trust, whether it's a non-disclosure agreement or understanding that certain information doesn't leave the room. Remember Ryan's fight club? Setting clear boundaries prevents issues down the line and ensures everyone knows they are expected to act with integrity.

No insults, rudeness, or putting down the competition.
Nothing breaks down collaboration faster than negativity. In successful collaborations, there is no room for rudeness, insults, or put downs. Stick to the age-old adage of "think before you speak."

Do not mistake this rule for saying the room should be free of conflict. On the contrary, when people understand the difference between unnecessary negativity and truth telling, trust is built. Trust is the foundation for positive conflict, which can result in great resolutions and solutions. Know the difference.

Establish core values. When collaborating within your business, establishing company core values is a fantastic way to make sure everyone is participating with integrity and grace. If you don't have core values and things go wrong, it's very hard to fix the problem because you can't reign people back or hold them accountable to a set of standards.

At Little Bird Marketing, we have four core values:

1. CARE DEEPLY
   We care deeply about our own advancement, the client's work, our colleagues' workloads, and our colleagues' work. In everything we do, we care

deeply because how you do anything is how you do everything.

2. FINISH STRONG

   Anybody can get a project started, but if it is worth starting, then it is worth finishing. We deliver at the same level of care, diligence, and attention to detail from beginning to end.

3. STAY GOLD

   Our brand takes pride in being known as best in class. This means we are best at work, best on planes, best in conference rooms, etc. Excellence is baked into our brand in how we show up, bring our all, and hold ourselves to high standards without exception.

4. BE TRUE

   We operate with integrity. We speak the truth without putting down a competitor, a client, co-worker, or ourselves. We report our actions transparently and spend client budgets like it was our own money.

Regardless of whether a collaboration is personal or corporate, core values need to be spoken and in alignment. If they don't align, you likely won't be able to establish common ground rules, and it might be best to step away from the collaboration.

THE FRAMEWORK

Three things create the framework for possible collaboration:

1. Everyone must be able to articulate what they have to win and what they have to lose.

2. Everyone must be willing to work without hidden agendas.

3. Everyone must have a desire to fight for the win.

To get you thinking about the best way to develop your own framework, here are some questions to consider:

- What do I have to give?

- What does each person stand to lose and gain?

- What is each person's approach, skills, level of expertise, and resources?

- How complex is the problem? Does it really require collaboration?

- What am I trying to really solve? How am I sure that this is the problem that I need to solve?

- What would it look like if I got the right people at the table?

How do you know when you need more ground rules, or that you need to revisit them? Look for these tell-tale signs. Then address them:

- People don't have an equal say.

- There are no consequences for things not getting done.

- Frustration is a key emotion of every gathering.

- Someone is constantly being talked over—or is the one interrupting others.

- People aren't on time for meetings, or they skip them completely.

- People who don't attend aren't missed.

Once you've established a strong framework and ground rules with your collaborators, though, it's time to have fun.

A CLOSER LOOK:
MARKET RESEARCH COLLAB

During the global pandemic, Sarah Kotva, Executive Vice President of Fieldwork, Inc., and her team were struggling because their work involves recruiting for and hosting in-person qualitative research. Because people couldn't meet face-to-face, they were suddenly doing only a fraction of their typical workload.

In the old way of thinking, Sarah would have asked my company to create ads to promote their brand and online qualitative technologies. Instead, she thought bigger. Her idea was to promote the industry as a whole instead of any single business. Many of the companies she approached were hesitant at first (who wouldn't be dubious about collaborating with their competitors?), but after some thought, they realized that if they worked together, they could stay afloat together.

Sarah became a thought leader in her industry by finding the bigger win through collaboration. She found others who had something to lose and something to gain. She asked if they would be willing to work together without hidden agendas. And she asked for a commitment in some combination of money or sweat equity—nailing all three requirements for successful collaboration. With the entire industry at risk, they came together, agreed to a framework, laid the ground rules and asked me to put together a collaborative ad campaign for them as a whole.

As a part of the campaign, the group together put out the hashtag #facetofaceMRX to generate a swell of awareness and interest in the in-person market research industry. For example, while brands could wait to test a new beverage product until it was safe to do so, life-saving product testing had to find a way to continue safely. This social media campaign helped the public appreciate what the face-to-face market research industry really does and the kind of support they needed when the name of the game was social distancing. It showcased powerful insights you can only get from in-person interaction and demonstrated their commitment to complying with CDC protocols.

Previously, such social media collaboration between competitors would not have seemed possible, but for Fieldwork and the other participating businesses, collaboration didn't mean sharing trade secrets. It meant aligning their agendas to save themselves. It meant putting a small amount of money into a collective pot, pooling resources and providing tangible tasks to show their drive to win.

When I stopped counting, #facetofaceMRX had been used over 100,000 times on social media, and despite the strain of the pandemic, all of the companies involved in the campaign survived. The same can't be said for those that didn't participate.

BRINGING INTENTION TO COLLABORATION

The purpose of creating a framework and ground rules isn't to make this process more complicated. Preparing this way encourages us to be intentional about our choices and actions versus following a corporate structure that dictates our careers, how we lead, and how we influence communities. If we choose to think, and choose to be intentional, we can make dynamic choices that solve multiple problems for multiple people all at once. That impact is the compounding benefit of engaging in true collaboration.

In our modern world, seven simple steps aren't enough to get us ahead. Companies aren't in charge anymore: consumers are. Business as usual is now unusual. To get the competitive edge, use a framework and ground rules to conduct business in a new way. Then cast your anchors.

Part Two

CASTING ANCHORS

"I am not afraid of storms for I am learning how to sail my ship."

—LOUISA MAY ALCOTT

I LOVE TO SAIL. THE SENSE OF ADVENTURE IS UNPARALLELED, and my husband is the ultimate captain, cook and bottle washer, so sailing journeys are a rather cushy endeavor for me. But all journeys require maps, charts and guideposts. You have to assume you will get lost, and that is the first step in preparing to get the help you need at critical times. When things don't go smoothly, it's best to cast an anchor somewhere safe to reassess your way forward.

Collaboration is a habit, and like all habits, it takes a little work to integrate collaboration into your life. Just as in sailing, we can encounter rough waters. These are the "anchors" I promised you in the introduction, which will give you a different way to address problems. You need to get out of the proverbial storm, navigate yourself somewhere safe, and cast an anchor to plot your next course.

But did you know that boats carry multiple anchors? This is a good metaphor because not all anchors are created equally. Some are made for muddy bottoms, others will find purchase on rocky outcrops, etc. You never know where you're going to need to stop and get a grip, so these anchors are not going to work in every situation. You might need to lower one down, try it out, and see if it holds. Likewise, these business "anchors" are for you to try out, see if they apply for your situation and use them as a tool.

We've all been conditioned to look at work a certain way (an anchor is an anchor is an anchor). But what if these anchors could give you options in tough situations and provide the right safe harbor, where you could discover new opportunities for collaboration? When you develop the habit of trying new anchors, you'll stumble into revelations about possible bigger wins and how you can make them a reality with less effort and more energy to continue the journey.

I offer you 7 anchors for when the seas get too rough, or the way is confused:

1. Always Be Helping

2. Itchy Backs

3. Digital First

4. Vice Versa

5. Uber or Lyft

6. Rule of 15

7. Be the Zebra

Put these anchors to work. Steal them, tweak them, and share them as tidbits that make you the most interesting person at the next cocktail party. Most importantly, *use them* to change the way you work. To get you out of the *I win, you lose* mindset, even beyond a simple *win-win* mindset, and into an expansive collaborative state of mind.

If you finish this book, set it down, and forget about it, you've missed the opportunity that could dramatically change your career, business, and life. Instead, put what you learned into practice and you'll break out of the habits that aren't serving you and go beyond the modes passed down from an outdated world.

But what do these anchors mean? Let's get started.

7

ALWAYS BE HELPING

20 minute read

IF YOU WANT TO SEE HOW WE USED TO CONDUCT SALES BACK in the day, just watch the famous "always be closing!" scene in *Glengarry Glen Ross*. In the movie, a group of low-performing sales representatives at a real estate firm compete against each other to make the most sales—and the loser gets fired.

Alec Baldwin's character, Blake, is a spot-on representation of a horrific salesperson. We cringe at Blake's behavior, but it was par for the course in sales for a long time. He flaunts his wealth, berates the team, and orders them to follow the ABC rule: *always be closing.*

The firm sends their top salesman (and back then, they were all sales*men*) to harass the team into performing better. A salesman goes to the back of the room to get a cup of coffee and Blake issues the famous line, "Put the coffee down! Coffee's for closers!"

The men rely on lying, cheating, and even stealing to secure more sales and keep their jobs, cementing the stereotype of sleazy salesmen who take advantage of their clients. It's a mindset of exploitation. This ABC tactic was the cornerstone of the old school sales approach. Salespeople would push their customers into a sale no matter what unethical tactics they needed to use to close.

This attitude toward sales is frightening, and why many people avoid salespeople whenever possible. It's almost painful for me to watch *Glengarry Glen Ross* because it's so antithetical to how consumers want to be treated.

THE ALWAYS BE HELPING ANCHOR

The "always be closing" mentality objectifies individuals into obstacles. Salespeople must overcome these obstacles in order to hit a sales number. Never once are they asked to consider what that person truly needs. While that objectification was the cornerstone of the old school sales approach, consumers aren't putting up with it anymore.

Consumers don't want to be thought of as mere, well, *consumers* anymore. They want to be treated like people. They're not faceless targets; they're individuals—parents, professionals, athletes, artists. They're not consuming—they're supporting their lives, and they want the motivations behind their purchases to be acknowledged.

Today, if businesses want to survive, they have to acknowledge that today's consumer holds the most power in sales. Here are a few truths about what the modern consumer wants:

People Want to Make Their Own Decisions

The ABC sales approach that has been built over generations doesn't work anymore. Nobody in their right mind goes to a used car lot on Saturday unless they really need a car. Nobody wants to answer the door for a salesman. Most consumers avoid salespeople at all costs.

Salespeople used to be involved right at the beginning of the sales process, even initiating it. They took every opportunity that life presented to make a sale and inserted themselves in the consumer's buying decision. Now the situation has flipped. The buyer can present the world with whatever they want and center themselves at the start of every buying decision.

And they know what they want—exactly what they want. After all, the average buyer is 57 percent of the way through the buying process before they contact a salesperson. By the time they meet the salesperson, they've already done their due diligence, anonymously researching the experts in the field and reviewing their offerings and personal brand without having to actually engage. The salesperson is no longer in control and is often clueless as to the initial leading indicators of a purchase.

Back in the day, if someone were interested in a boat, they would have to personally go to the marina and interact with salespeople, get brochures on a few different boats, and then take that information home. The consumer's purchase decision was significantly influenced by their interactions with salespeople.

Because of the internet, people can do all of their research and shopping impersonally online. The consumer does not have to engage personally with the business until, and unless, they want to.

Consumers can even do their own competitive recon and quickly look up all of the major competitors of a brand. In fact, anyone can simply Google who your exact competitor is and start evaluating your offerings against theirs on their own self-guided and anonymous buyer's journey. People are willing to take all of the responsibility for research because they don't want to interact with salespeople until absolutely necessary—often, never. The buyer has so much information at their fingertips, requiring so little investment of time and effort, that there's no reason to contact a salesperson until they're ready to make a purchase, and that only when they're buying something that requires direct interaction.

Consumers are also aware of sales techniques. They've learned how to skip past ads and intuitively understand even native advertising and editorial. Skepticism runs deep, so every attempt at connection—sad commercials about saving animals or children, campaigns that center social issues, ads that speak to the difficulties of parenting—is critiqued as pandering, and yet the consumer won't tolerate impersonal messaging that doesn't center on their values. They know how to filter clickbait, and many people use alternate email addresses for shopping to avoid the email advertising that often follows a purchase. Above all, we value and protect our anonymity.

People Want to be Left Alone

As the CEO of a digital marketing firm specializing in lead generation, I know full well what lengths people will go to in order to get valuable content but not be contacted. Avoiding one-sided, parasocial relationships with companies has become an artform.

I get it. I grew up in Europe, and I hate going out to dinner in the United States at restaurants where waiters are trained to use the ABC approach. As soon as you sit down, they give their name and launch into: "I'm going to be taking care of you tonight. How are you doing today? Are you here tonight for any special occasion?" I'm already exhausted, and I don't want to chat.

I don't expect servers to be rude, but I appreciate the European approach—they recognize I came to the restaurant for a particular reason and they honor that reason. They don't expect me to engage in banter and treat dinner as entertainment. They certainly don't sit down in the booth and tell me about their day or ask me about mine.

People avoid disingenuous relationships, and since COVID we've realized we don't even have to deal with people to get dinner. Even young people who can barely afford fast food are using food delivery apps and paying ten dollars extra for someone to deliver their food to them. That's how deep in-person sales avoidance runs in younger generations. They're not interested in being "sold."

People Want Out of Your Funnel

In the past, companies would run ads saying, "Give us your information and we'll give you a free guide on how to retire in Portugal!" Of course, I want the guide! But within minutes the phone rang and someone on the other end (most likely someone in another country reading a script in a call center) said, "I heard you want to retire in Portugal!" Then I was just dumped into some company's sales funnel, and there was no way out.

As a content marketing and lead generation expert, I knew what was next. I proceeded to be hounded, badgered, and annoyed, thanks to that one fleeting moment when Portugal seemed like a good idea. (Honestly, retiring to Portugal is still a good idea. I call dibs. But you get my point that I learned an important lesson in salesperson avoidance.)

In the ABC approach to sales, there's no nurturing of the relationship between company and consumer. The funnel is short, and the company using it takes the consumer from the awareness stage straight to the decision. Today, people don't want to be shoved through your funnel. They refuse to be pushed, and though we won't be abandoning sales funnels anytime soon, we do have to learn to respect the stage the customer is in within that funnel.

Are you willing to give up some of your expertise before they commit to buying? If you can't answer yes, don't expect collaboration between yourself and your prospective customer to succeed. And don't be surprised when they block your number, mark your email as spam, and never visit your website again no matter how many retargeting campaigns you run.

People Want to be Helped

People want someone who will actually help them. If they're just gathering information, can you be the one to help?

To always be helping, forget about pitching features and benefits consumers don't care about. It's a waste of time, yet salespeople still use these tactics.

Again, recall the last time you visited a car lot: the salesperson probably peppered you with features and benefits of some car you didn't want that had features you didn't need. "These automatic seats will improve your life! This media system is exactly what you need! If I can prove this, will you buy it?" *Of course not, because that's not my goal and it doesn't solve my problem. Maybe I don't want four-wheel drive, but I do need room for car seats.*

Consumers want sellers to understand their needs and truly connect with them on a personal level, instead of pitching as many angles as possible and hoping one of them will stick. Consumers don't want to be subjected to bait-and-switch tactics. They want sellers to shut up and listen.

Effective sales approaches that truly connect with the consumer's persona understand two things: What are the persistent problems that the person is facing, and what are the newly emerging problems in that person's life? Successful companies know how to address either (or both) of these and share their expertise in a scalable way to build rapport and prove that they can be trusted.

The truth is that no matter how good you are at your job, you have to earn that trust with the customer. By giving away your expertise early in the game, you can insert yourself earlier into the customer's journey, thereby giving you a competitive advantage.

Instead of ABC, always be closing, shift to the anchor ABH— Always Be Helping.

BE A RESOURCE

The ABH, Always Be Helping, anchor is more than wanting to help the consumer figure out the problem they're facing. To truly create a relationship, companies need to help customers satisfy their values and their hidden needs.

For example, I may publish a blog post about the Pomodoro technique and how it can create better productivity and get more reward out of your time. I don't sell productivity resources—I sell digital marketing expertise and systems—but this builds rapport and helps my ideal client persona, who is busy. They come across a resource they can use, notice that I care about their needs, and ask, "What are you selling, again?" They are interested in me and my products and services because I showed interest in *them*.

Think of the old adage, *People don't care how much you know until they know how much you care.* People want the companies they buy from to care about the same things they care about.

Some businesses have been able to maintain a balance between satisfying people's hidden agenda, or their values, and working in a way that doesn't align with them. For example, a company may be vilified because of their collection of personal data, but they also may meet the values of their ideal clients by being carbon neutral. They know that their consumers might not like some things they do, but they know how to showcase their clients' values in a way that builds rapport.

Understand Your Customer's Preferences

Part of building rapport is understanding how not to break trust with the consumer. People don't tolerate impersonal or tone deaf marketing. Instead of being talked at, they want to be understood. To a large degree, consumers are voting with their wallets.

Technology has driven us further down the rabbit hole of the consumer-driven sales process. Many people, including myself, pay more for streaming services and ad-free packages so they don't have to be exposed to commercials that have taken over cable TV. I haven't had network TV since I was seventeen years old; I've paid extra for subscriptions without ads for thirty years. People used to say I was an outlier—but not anymore. My whole entertainment media consumption is an ad-free experience, which is hilarious considering I'm the CEO of a digital advertising and marketing company.

I know that the customers I have to reach feel the same way. Of course, if someone gives me something of undeniable value, I will sacrifice my anonymity and let them contact me. But the moment they break that trust, I'm out. And I'm not alone.

For example, when I went on a cruise last year, I signed up for pertinent information regarding my trip. Do you know how often they emailed me? Every. Single. Day. I don't want to consider going on a cruise every single day of my life, so I finally blocked the email. Maybe I would've kept that relationship going if they had sent me something of value, such as an update about upcoming trips and new itineraries. Instead, I was accosted with daily offers I didn't ask for and didn't find relevant. In what way was constantly harassing me to spend more money building rapport or helping me?

Just as annoying as rote, unhelpful advertising is the constant push for surveys. There's nothing wrong with surveys, but there's a time and a place for them. And if you're not going to actually take them into account and respond to your customers' needs, then what's the point? The customer's job isn't to manage how you're doing, and they really don't want to fill out a survey every time they buy a pair of socks.

It's important that brands stay in the loop with what their consumers want, but it has to be done in ways that don't break their trust. A "closing tactic" disguised as faux helpfulness is forcing a relationship with the customer. Consider how to operate from the ABH mindset when asking for feedback. Instead of asking every single customer about their experience every single time, maybe ask a select group.

It all comes down to not disrespecting the consumer by being insensitive or objectifying them. Treat them as humans, not targets—because you'd appreciate the same respect.

Understand Your Customer's Values

Consumers are driving major businesses into doing things differently. They want to self-direct their own buying experience and are driven by their own values.

For example, people have certain values around sustainability and eco-friendliness. They want a product, and you might offer the best and cheapest product, but now they want to know if you share their values, and they want to know if those shared values are evident in your brand and even in the product. Industries can no longer make decisions based solely on the fact that customers need a product and what they're willing to pay to get it. Now, brands have a long list of consumer values they need to understand that are the key drivers behind purchases.

Consumers want to feel heard and seen, and brands have to pay attention if they want to stay afloat. And it's not only what customers tell you that matters—they also have hidden agendas, those things that matter to them that they may not be telling you.

For example, in 1996 when it came out that Kathie Lee Gifford's clothing line was produced from sweatshop labor, there was a huge public uproar against the brand. It didn't matter that many other clothing brands were doing the same thing. Her brand got singled out and the company changed their practices. Other clothing brands took notice and did the same. This incident raised awareness of changing customer values and the new concerns over production that are now at the forefront of consumers' minds. Now, social responsibility and sustainability are a cornerstone of many clothing brands' messaging.

Values matter, and the success of companies like Chick-fil-A back this up. The company promotes a culture of positivity and a "My pleasure!" attitude toward service. They give their employees Sunday off, which appeals to some religious customers. People who share Chick-fil-A's values support them, praise them, and buy more chicken. No chicken sandwich is that much more special than other chicken sandwiches, but the company has won the hearts and minds of consumers because of their values.

On the other hand, Chick-fil-A has also turned many consumers off because of their political views and employee benefits. This doesn't mean your brand shouldn't have strong values; after all, the moment that a brand tries to be everything to everyone is when they become nothing to no one. But understanding your ideal client's values means you can more effectively help the clients you want to attract, while repelling those who aren't relevant to your business.

Share Expertise

You have to prove your expertise before you get buy-in for what you're offering. From years of teaching social selling to B2B professionals and reading countless research reports, I know that buyers are looking to work with someone who they perceive as an expert in their field. Besides creating personal rapport with a consumer, sharing expertise also sets you up as a leader in your industry.

For example, my LinkedIn account says that I'm a marketer, but how do I prove that I'm any good? First, I have a lot of recommendations from clients over many years. Second, my content is overtly helpful. Third, I've written hundreds of free resources.

Not everyone wants to pay me to do high-end strategy for them, which is fine by me. There's no reason I can't share tips and information with people who can't afford what I do in order to increase my influence. I showcase my expertise by strategically giving it away.

Giving something away in no way dilutes what I offer for a fee. The people who can afford my services don't want my free stuff anyway because they want the personalized, strategic expertise I offer. In both cases, I'm speaking to my niche audience and finding ways to connect. I do a lot more showing than telling, letting my most ideal client discover my expertise for themselves.

Create Content to Connect

When you are building your content, make sure some of it is enticing, and some is refining. I don't want to pitch to people who aren't a match for my services, but to those who are genuinely interested.

Content should attract your ideal clients naturally, rather than forcibly targeting people. When you try to hard-sell people, you don't learn anything about them. You don't even know if they're a potential customer or not, so you're wasting your time and theirs.

My most important tip about building content and attracting your ideal clients is that you can't be everything for everyone. People will self-select whether they find your content valuable or not. This builds an engaged audience of people who actually care about your expertise and want to stick around for more, and they'll keep doing so until they reach out and say, "I love what you're doing. How can I work with you?"

When you connect with your ideal clients, you don't have to close because the customers close themselves. Moving from ABC to ABH means shifting from forced closure to incentivizing the customer to close because they're a part of your specific, targeted audience and have discovered for themselves that your product or service is right for them.

I can't even tell you the last time I went in for a close because it was that long ago. Seriously—and my business is better for it. It's the customer's decision, and you're helping them on their path to purchase instead of pushing them to the finish line. When you're walking beside them, that's the ABH mindset in action.

Achieve Bigger Wins

It might sound counterintuitive, but when you stop trying to sell someone and collaborate instead, you'll see bigger wins. That's because you'll be able to focus on bigger problems than simply beating the competition; the key is that you'll no longer be driven by the ABC mindset. Take your mind off closing, and you'll be able to enter into true collaboration, generated from an expansive motivation to help your ideal client.

Collaboration doesn't stop at the individual level. Many times when I'm trying to solve a client's problem, I'll recognize where I need to bring more people to the table, such as booking contracts from other vendors for the benefit of my client. When I bring more people into collaboration, I'm not trying to sell their stuff, either; I'm creating more wins by looking out for the best interests of my client and myself.

Create a Genuine Connection

Unfortunately, a lot of salespeople have learned only the "language" of collaboration. They'll say things like, "Let me listen and see if I'm a good fit," but then they go in for the kill and try to sell the client, whose problems fall on deaf ears.

True collaboration is saying, "I might not be the right person to offer direction, but I'm willing to listen and offer my help." Be sincere that a "no" from your customer is okay because you're willing to trade an hour of your time for the sake of working with your ideal client. Also, be upfront if you can't help in the way they need. After I give potential clients an hour of my time, I tell them that I'm not going to aggressively follow up with them. Instead, I let them know that if they feel like my services are worth the conversation, they can contact me.

By giving away your time, you take a risk, but you'll never know if you're the solution a potential customer is looking for unless you are willing to collaborate from the start. You might not be the solution, and that's okay, because you're not selling. You're solving.

After I've given potential clients an hour and they recognize that there's something there, we're both willing to invest a few more hours of our time and create a productive, profitable relationship. I have something to lose and gain, and so does the customer. Trying to close your customer means that you don't value their time.

Still, I'm not going to pretend like I'm *not* selling something, because that would waste my time. But I respect my customers by not focusing on closing them. When you seek to help them first, you enter into collaboration that results in bigger wins; collaboration breeds more collaboration—and more opportunity for sales.

ABH IS NOT ALTRUISM

Sales shouldn't be a dirty word; of course everyone's goal is to make a sale so that they can put food on the table. Similarly, ABH should not be dismissed as altruism in which you give and give without any reward.

When I lead by helping others, I'm getting exactly what I want *and* I get paid for my work. I want clients who appreciate what I can offer, who value my expertise and are willing to pay top dollar for it, but I'm not going to act like one of us serves the other because we both serve each other. Treating people the ABH way invites collaboration.

At the same time, I recognize when not to invest more time for the sake of a shallow and unfulfilling relationship. It's fine if I'm not the right person for a potential client because I can then turn my focus to my most ideal client.

To work this way, you have to be willing to show your cards, but people have learned the hard way not to show their cards too early in the game. For example, someone might need a new SUV, but they hide their agenda from the car salesman so that they aren't pushed into a purchase. Collaboration requires trust, which is built on rapport. You'll know you've entered into real collaboration when everyone feels safe enough to reveal rather than withhold their cards.

It's possible to be upfront about being a salesperson without defaulting to closing or falling into altruism. Surprise: used car dealerships aren't non-profits. For everyone to get exactly what they want, everyone has to be upfront about their hidden agendas; then, we can do the sale in a fraction of the time instead of engaging in this unproductive dance in which one side always loses.

At the end of the day, a consumer will only choose you above everyone else when they realize you're the one who is willing to help them instead of sell them. Sharing your expertise lets the consumer know you're done with disingenuous relationships and hidden agendas. When you prove that not only do you have what the consumer needs, but you won't break their trust, you'll spend more time doing the real work at the heart of your business instead of chasing after customers who don't truly value what you offer.

A CLOSER LOOK:
PONDERINGS FROM THE PERCH

I started my podcast *Ponderings from the Perch* to connect with people and build my personal brand. I never thought I'd make any money from it, and I was never trying to sell something. Now, tens of thousands of downloads and 350 episodes later, I've built a platform that makes it easy to lead by helping, by inviting someone to engage with my audience on my podcast. If there's someone I would love to have in my network, I have this tool at the ready to help me make that connection.

When I reach out, I usually say something like, "I'd really love to amplify your thought leadership. Would you like to be featured on an episode of my podcast? I'd love to host you." When I lead with giving, people find it hard to turn me down.

When I needed someone to speak at Insights Marketing Day, for example, I called my friend and author Michael Brenner, who has been on my podcast twice. The catch was that I didn't have any money for the event. He said that he would be happy to give me that favor, but he couldn't make the date work.

Dang. That wasn't really what I was looking for. The good news is that authors know other authors, so I said, "Well, do you know someone else who might be a good fit? I can't pay them a speaking fee, but could cover one night at a hotel, buy fifty books from them, feature them on my podcast, and give them a stage in front of my carefully curated audience."

Michael introduced me to Len Herstein, the author of *Be Vigilant!: Strategies to Stop Complacency, Improve Performance, and Safeguard Success. Your Business and Relationships Depend on It.* He agreed to be a speaker on my stage.

In the meantime, I got a call from Meta because they were interested in being featured on another podcast I had created called *Digital Transformation Success.* Underwriting for that podcast costs $12,000, and there is value in that transaction. But if I had seen only that perspective I would have lost out on a bigger collaboration.

The truth is that I would get more out of someone from Meta being on my show than they would, being one of the big five American information technology companies. Business as usual would leave me with one nice payday but nothing else. Instead, I offered them two podcast interview spots and asked them to foot the travel bill to come to Austin and speak on my Insights Marketing Day stage. They said yes.

I didn't get cash from that collaboration, but I got a major name that drew a bigger audience to my event. However, the best part was being able to turn around and tell Len, who was gracious enough to drive himself to the conference and not charge a speaker fee, "Guess what? You're sharing the stage with Meta." I got the benefit of having his authority *and* Meta's at the conference and on my podcast. Len got exposure and the extra draw of sharing a stage with Meta. And Meta got their own podcast feature and a speaking opportunity. This is exponential wins through collaborative thinking and action.

When you lead with helping, bring the right people with something to win and something to lose to the table and ask for full disclosure of what everyone wants and needs while the collaborative process is in play. Being open to seeing the situation differently leads to bigger opportunities where more are helped and you will be helped in return—often more than you could ever expect.

DEVELOPING AN ABUNDANCE MENTALITY... AND SOME BOUNDARIES

As powerful as it is to lead with an ABH mentality, you'll sometimes be dealing with people who still operate under the ABC paradigm. Creating boundaries for how we conduct business prevents us from being surprised when we give an inch and others take a mile.

I've learned not to engage in relationships where people continue to rely on the ABC mindset. After all, relationships aren't one-sided. I have agency, and I can leave. Otherwise, if I keep working with them, I'm being complicit. Allowing that behavior to continue is signaling that it works, and they'll continue to ABC other people.

Don't walk into the bar, or onto a car lot, with people who hide their agendas, expect blind altruism, or have a scarcity mentality. Admit that you have something to lose and something to gain and expect the same from your collaborators, leveraging an abundance mentality.

To choose ABH over ABC, you have to believe that you have an abundance of expertise to give. Giving someone three pieces of marketing advice doesn't mean you won't be able to pay your bills for that month. You have expertise in abundance; sharing it doesn't diminish you at all. In fact, it attracts more abundance, setting you apart as a thought leader, providing more opportunities for collaboration, and creating bigger wins.

ITCHY BACKS

11 minute read

WE'VE ALL HAD THAT ONE ITCH WE COULDN'T SCRATCH. YOU know what I'm talking about. You feel like a dog wearing a cone, with an itch behind your ear that you just... can't... reach.

Imagine a room full of people who all have itchy backs, trying to scratch them on their own, going around and around in a strange, jerky, out-of-sync dance. Finally, one person gets the bright idea of trading back scratches with someone else. Everyone else catches on, and soon that jerky dance becomes a graceful, synchronized circle of people all scratching, and all having their backs scratched.

Scratching your own back is hard. So is trying to solve all your problems by yourself. It's much easier if two people, or three or more, are willing to help each other out, while simultaneously all getting exactly what they need.

You're probably thinking about that little itch behind your ear, or the big itch in the middle of your back. I want you to get clear about what you need scratched. Now hold that thought.

It's time to look for other people's itches.

THE ITCHY BACK ANCHOR

Cultivating your itchy-back radar is the quickest and easiest path to collaboration. Look around for people who need their backs scratched, who might be able to help you with your itch.

Unless you've developed your radar for identifying itchy backs, you won't see them. We're all so focused on our own problems, we're quick to dismiss other people's problems without considering for a moment how we might help. But itchy backs are everywhere. After many years of collaborating, I'm still surprised by how often these opportunities show up.

When someone shares a need they have, don't swoop in and start solving. Take a step back and remove yourself from the fix-it mentality that so many of us have adopted over years of delivering quick, shallow results. Instead of slapping a patch on the problem, consider how you might discover a better, deeper, longer-lasting solution. A big win for them, and maybe for you too. Maybe for more than just the two of you. Think about how you can collaborate to scratch more itchy backs—including your own.

For example, a few years ago I spoke at SampleCon, a convention for the consumer data industry. I kicked off the conference with the concept of collaboration and then got interactive with the audience to show them how it works. Later, the conversation turned to the low retention rate of junior staffers and how kids these days (read that with a grain of salt) don't stay long enough in the industry. Their companies were having a hard time because by the time they got junior staff trained in eight or ten months, they were off to something else.

Another firm mentioned that they have development programs for junior staff, but that they somehow couldn't get them interested in the program. Junior staff didn't understand how they could make it from one position to another, so after ten months they were leaving. A competitor said that some of those employees who left that competitor found themselves at their company, but after a few months, they were off again. In another room, I talked to someone at a foundation that worked with many young people who were struggling to break into better paying positions than the introductory roles they had landed after college.

All of these itchy backs were sitting next to each other in my audience. So many people with interrelated itches—what if I could get them all together to collaborate on a solution? Mind you, this wasn't as altruistic as it sounds. I was there as a speaker, trying to make a name for myself in the industry as a thought leader. If I could connect these different people and help them collaborate, that would go a long way toward scratching the big itch that was growing in the middle of my back too.

I brought the individuals together and our conversation led to the realization that people new to our industry struggled because the industry is hard to understand. It took time for entry-level staff to get comfortable in their positions, and once they had, they wanted to move up. However, our industry didn't offer a lot of opportunities to move up, so people simply jumped ship.

My connection at the foundation taught junior colleagues in the industry the basic job skills needed to kick off their careers. What if the experienced people at the companies they were leaving stuck around instead, with the incentive of training and mentoring new employees? What if the foundation provided a steady stream of these new people who wanted to break into the industry but were having trouble finding employment because of the steep learning curve?

These people from different companies and organizations realized that by collaborating, they could solve each other's problems. By entertaining the idea that they had something to win and something to lose if they collaborated, instead of focusing solely on their own itchy backs, they were able to solve a major problem and achieve multiple wins. Maybe it's unusual for two competitors to be in the same room solving the same problem, but when they have a problem that can't be solved alone, why wouldn't they give a little to get a lot?

How desperate are you to get your back scratched? Are you willing to reach across the aisle? You might have a chance to improve an entire industry.

Be the Connector

All of these companies with related problems were dying of an itch they couldn't reach while standing with people who could scratch it. They needed someone to connect them—someone to speak with all of them and say, "Well, it's funny that you said that, because I just heard stories from other people who have the same problem."

Even though everyone had similar problems, the solution wasn't one they could come up with on their own. I knew that if so many of the forty companies at that convention were experiencing the same issue, it was likely affecting people industry-wide. All I had to do was seek out the people from those industries who were most likely impacted and connect them.

What if all forty of those companies got together, put up a little bit of money, and came up with a small primer for junior people in the sample industry? If everyone put in just $1,000 and created a $40,000 initiative to train people up, wouldn't everyone get their $1,000 back—and then some? That's the collaborative opportunity they were all missing because they were thinking individually. On an individual level, they didn't have the budgets to create such an initiative, but collectively, they did.

To get that win, they couldn't approach the problem as a winner at the expense of losers. Each would have to give up a little bit of control and be willing to let other people join in the winning. They'd have to get vulnerable and share their needs. They would have to work with others with skin in the game— equally incentivised to solve the problem.

There can't be winners and losers anymore. Everyone has to win, and everyone has to have something to gain and lose for collaboration to happen. Not only that, but there needs to be a connector to recognize when opportunities exist for backs to be scratched.

Be that connector. Train yourself to see those itchy backs.

Turn on Your Itchy-back Radar

When we focus solely on our own problems, we aren't able to see the needs of others. We get into this weird mindset believing that other people's problems are other people's problems, and they have nothing to do with us. To find opportunities to collaborate, we need to pay attention, be aware, and ask the right questions. We must see life as "curiouser and curiouser..."

We all know the age-old advice for married couples: when your spouse says they have a problem, they don't want you to fix it. They just want you to listen. When you truly listen to others closely enough and ask probing questions, you can get to the heart of the matter. When people—including people at companies, and especially people at competing companies—don't listen to each other, they miss the opportunity to see how much they have, if not in common, in adjacency.

Instead of looking for collaboration opportunities, we look for patterns. Unfortunately, the pattern most of us have been trained to see looks like this: 1) I have a problem; 2) I fix the problem; 3) I repeat.

Once you turn on that itchy-back radar, I promise you, you will begin to see itchy backs everywhere. It's the bell that cannot be unrung—the pattern that cannot be unseen. You will wonder how you never saw them before when there they are, in plain sight, staring at you and begging to be scratched.

Change your mindset. Find other itchy backs and explore the possibility of working together to innovate a solution that has exponential wins. Ask questions to uncover other people's problems. Don't be embarrassed to ask those uncomfortable questions, thinking you're the only one with a problem. Everyone has issues, and if their itchy-back radar was turned on, they would be asking you questions.

To create bigger wins, stand up, be strong, and actively participate. Be willing to say, "So what's going on in your business? Tell me more." Get familiar with these questions. You can use them on the fly, or workshop them if there is someone in particular you want to collaborate with. Don't forget that you may need to print the worksheet out several times depending on the number of people you want to include in the collaboration!

Ask others:

- What's keeping you up at night?

- Who within my sphere of influence has a related issue?

- What do you want, and how can I deliver it?

- If we wanted to help each other, what would that look like?

- What is that elusive outcome you dream about?

- And ask yourself:

- How are their issues/wants/goals/needs adjacent to mine?

- What could I get out of a collaboration with them?

- Who else do I know who has an adjacent or related issue?

- Who do I think could help both of us?

Being the connector is about more than asking questions, though. It's also about letting go of hierarchy so that you can really listen to the answers. And that cuts both ways. If you've been in business 2 years or 20 years, you can still offer something meaningful.

Step Off Your Hierarchy

In El Salvador, the way to say you're welcome is *"para servirte,"* which translates to "Here to serve you." What if we went into interactions with the intention to serve someone? Couldn't serving be mutual? I served them; they served me. We can both walk away from that conversation trying to serve, and therefore create a bigger win, instead of thinking only about what's in it for us. The extremes of selfishness or altruism are both limited and limiting.

Break out of the dichotomized mindset that there's either the helper or helpee, the winner or loser. That mindset means that there's rarely an equal playing field. When a friend mentions a problem they're having, most people go into fixing mode because we operate on that unequal hierarchy.

As a CEO, if I'm talking to someone who is a brand new insight manager, I'm automatically socially trained to think that since I'm in the higher position, I should be solving something and contributing my wisdom. *That's not careful listening,* and it has nothing to do with collaboration. I need something as equally as this other person does, and I should find that inter- section instead of imposing a hierarchy that isn't conducive to collaboration.

How many collaborations could we create if we stopped sepa- rating ourselves? Of course, that's not going to work in every situation where collaboration isn't needed, such as in the case of a mentor and mentee relationship. But when we go into interactions believing that neither one of us is over the other, we could both get something out of the relationship.

Look for people that you can help, knowing that this service isn't altruistic because there's something you're getting out of it as well. Don't be afraid to get something out of a relationship because you have something to give. The catch is that in order to receive, you have to be open to giving.

If I give someone an hour of my time and we come to the conclusion that my services aren't the right fit, but they valued my advice, there's no reason why I can't say, "You know what? Our services aren't for everybody, and I understand if you're not in a position to hire us at the moment. Out of curiosity, is there someone else who you do think I would be a good fit for? Would you be willing to make that introduction for me? I'm happy to have given you that hour, but if our services are not right for you, I've got to find the person."

They might realize that they really valued that one hour and are willing to make that connection. It's about equity in honoring what each person needs. They don't need my services, which is fine, and I honor that by not putting them in a sales funnel. However, maybe that hour could be valuable for both of us if I get a referral out of it. Then, they're the connector— just like I was at the convention.

A CLOSER LOOK: CREATING A SPACE FOR ITCHY BACKS

After listening to people at conference after conference, I realized that it is easier to make the connections about similar issues when you're not behind a computer and in the weeds with your day-to-day job duties. But how do you leave an industry conference and keep this openness alive? I invited interested parties to join a casual "content pod" where these connections would agree to spend 1 hour each looking at each others' thought leadership and asks online. The idea is to intentionally read and support others' posts with the added lens of looking for commonalities and identify opportunities for collaboration.

I've done this more formally in the past by creating content pods with a set membership. After creating this free project management board on Trello, I invited eight industry colleagues and requested that they participate for a six month stint for greater accountability. Some of them didn't know each other, so I connected them. I said, "Look, we're not going to do business with each other or trade money, but we could help each other with one thing that's of value to all of us: online engagement." We went into collaboration with the intent to serve each other by liking, commenting on, and promoting each other's online content. Along the way, we would experience what it feels like to be honest with colleagues and competitors about what we need while scratching others' backs in an efficient way.

We organized all of our social media handles onto one board for quick reference. The idea was that in order to participate in the content pod, each person had to come to the monthly meeting, which was forty minutes, and spend another forty minutes sometime during the month helping someone else. Everyone would share the most important thing for them that month—*I need you to promote this. I'm launching a project on this date. I'm speaking at this event, can you talk about it?*—and we would each help with that one thing.

It was a small contribution, but that's eight people giving 80 minutes per month to understand and promote something important to someone else. It felt genuine and at times serendipitous while still having clear expectations, spanning an entire industry, and having an expiration date.

STOP, COLLABORATE, AND LISTEN

To collaborate, we need to take a page from Vanilla Ice's "Ice Ice Baby" by stopping and listening. We need to reframe how we seek and offer service to others.

Looking for itchy backs goes beyond the fix-it mentality. We're conditioned to have a problem and solve it on our own, but this one-on-one back-scratching is antithetical to finding opportunities for collaboration and experiencing bigger wins.

To collaborate, we need to reframe how we seek and offer service to others. Break out of your limited perspective and realize that if you found three people who have adjacent problems, you'd get three times the impact that you could create alone.

DIGITAL FIRST

17 minute read

WRITING THIS BOOK IN 2023, I'M THINKING ABOUT HOW the last three years felt like an involuntary book club, where everyone's reading the mystery novel *COVID and The Case of the Shrinking Network*. Everyone wants to know how it ends, but each time we think we've finished the book, another chapter is there for us to push our way through. It's exhausting, I know, but the fact of the matter is that we were already heading toward a digital business landscape. COVID just made it apparent how prepared—or more often, unprepared people were when our digital presence became the most important lifeboat for modern business strategy.

The way we work was turned upside down, but I had an advantage because of how immersed I was in the digital business landscape. In fact, when I first learned about COVID, I was in Amsterdam speaking about the transformational power of digital platforms. My timing couldn't have been better.

Business has been tipping more and more into the digital world. I'm not an oracle or psychic, but I was aware of this not-so-secret shift and had already learned how to leverage the digital space. It's revolutionized how we connect, how we work, and how we present ourselves to the world. Most importantly, a digital first strategy creates a wealth of opportunities that we'd otherwise never have.

THE DIGITAL FIRST ANCHOR

If you're not currently and actively engaged in pulling digital transformation across your entire organization, you don't know it yet, but someone's eating your lunch. You're behind. Going digital with your network isn't a thing of the future. It's not even a thing of the present. It's a thing of the past. This shouldn't be groundbreaking news, but if it is, you need to start moving.

We're no longer in the days of getting our news from the town crier or the paper boy on the street corner yelling, "Read all about it!" News doesn't even spread around the water cooler like it used to when people would actually stand around and have conversations. That's all changed, and it's changed quickly thanks to the pandemic. Now, news arrives directly on my phone. I don't even have to ask for the news and my phone automatically tells me. I can't help but stay up to date with the news—I'd have to actively un-pursue it.

That's how our society has progressed. Let's look now at how our work has progressed.

Once upon a time, we had a little black book of contacts. Then we got really sophisticated and used Rolodexes. Then came Palm pilots that carried a lot more than a Rolodex and fit in your back pocket. Our networks kept growing, but at some point there was a limit. We could only connect with so many people face-to-face.

What we now know, thanks to developers like Mark Zuckerberg, is that we don't have to be limited. We can grow our connections exponentially on a platform someone else has created—regardless of who really created it in the first place.

We came up with more sophisticated ways to be social, and we've also created sophisticated ways to be more purposeful about who we want to meet. After all, even though turn-of-the-century doomsayers thought the internet was going to kill society, people are still going to be social. Humans are social beings. I mean, *the telegraph* was social media.

Now, it's simply much easier—and faster—to make the connections we want to make. In the past, I had a wish list of the top twenty companies that I wanted to work with, and it took my whole life to find somebody who knew somebody who knew somebody (ad nauseum) who worked at one of those companies; once that connection was there, it took forever to network through that tangle of relationships. These days, I can go onto LinkedIn and within two minutes find someone at one of these companies and connect with them.

Case in point, as a small company I'm basically a nobody to huge corporations, and yet because I've leveraged digital connections, within one week I talked with someone at Hershey's, Coke, Mars, BET, MTV, and three people at Meta. Because of digital connectivity, these companies are open to making connections online instead of me calling them directly and hoping for a response that might never come. They want to be engaged online and actively network, even with people at small companies like mine.

Recently, my esteemed colleague Bianca at BET responded to my LinkedIn message, we became friends, and she was featured on my podcast. I emailed her about a panel, and when she was unavailable, she told me about her contact Tara at Indeed who lives in Austin. With a quick email, that connection was instantly made.

Without this digital connection, how long would it have taken me to meet someone meaningfully from Indeed? It probably would've taken me driving to the office, trying to get through the door, and being turned away by security. Impossible, outside of stalking, if it weren't for digital connectivity.

The reality is that we can connect with *anybody*. Well, I wouldn't say anybody, but almost anyone. Think of it like the six degrees of Kevin Bacon, in which everyone can come within six connections of knowing Kevin Bacon himself. In this case, it's the six degrees of Will Ferrell because I once worked with him at Wells Fargo as a teller. You now know me because you're holding this book. If you think about everyone Will Ferrell has ever met, you're probably two connections away from almost everyone.

That's not how our world was before. Before, we could only connect and keep meaningful connections with maybe a few dozen people, and even the highest connectors could only have maybe two hundred people max they really knew and were able to keep in touch with. Now, we can maintain thousands.

I have well over ten thousand connections on LinkedIn, and I'm a bit choosy. If I were to really try, I could probably have thirty thousand LinkedIn connections, but if a connection doesn't make sense, I don't invest in that relationship. I make the most of LinkedIn as a social platform, but I use it intentionally.

On LinkedIn, I always lead with helping people and seeing how I can help without them having to give anything in return. For example, I have two podcasts as a way to be of service, and I don't expect my listeners to give something back. Even so, my podcast has opened plenty of collaboration opportunities for myself and my business because I chose to leverage the digital platform to my advantage.

That's not to say that social media is the magical networking solution. Silos remain, because people tend to stick with people they already know and agree with; even when they go to conferences and meet people face-to-face, they don't have new conversations. They often just rehash the same old problems and solutions. Everyone is in avoidance mode. News, ideas, and game-changing conversations can't spread within a silo. In order to collaborate, you have to escape the silo.

Today's conversations aren't taking place at the water cooler, but happening online via social and professional networking sites. The risk is that silos will remain, and be strengthened. But the opportunity is there to start new conversations with new people, on a new scale. This is the future of work.

Collaboration begins with taking the initiative to start conversations. Reach out to others, post your original ideas, and invite others into the conversation. When you operate from an abundance mindset and use digital platforms as a launch pad, you'll create opportunities far bigger than you could have ever imagined.

HOW TO LEVERAGE DIGITAL TRANSFORMATION

Going digital first means that you're no longer focused on the logistical limitations of trying to connect in person with all of the people you want to meet. Not only can you easily connect with others with a simple comment, but you can also create *intentional* connections.

Unlike a typical day in the office when people would talk about many different things and get distracted from the one task, problem, or big idea at hand, communication is no longer interruptive. In the digital arena, you can clearly indicate what your priorities are and find those who are willing to help you find the right solution.

International Affairs

If you still don't believe just how powerful going digital first is, let me give you a personal example of how it's changed my business—online and in real life.

Years ago, I was heading to London to speak at a conference. I wasn't getting paid to be there, but I wanted to become an international speaker so I accepted the offer because I knew it would be great for my business. Going all the way to London for one conference and turning right around to come home wasn't an efficient use of my time, so I decided to leverage my online network to make it worthwhile.

I reached out to ten friends and acquaintances online that were in senior positions above mine. I told them, "I'm going to London because I have a speaking opportunity, and I really need to build some international connections. You know me, I'm pretty fun and not a jerk. If you will connect me to a couple people in your industry who you think would hit it off with me, I'll promise you three things. Number one, that I won't try to sell them anything. Two, that I won't take up more than an hour of their time. Three, that I will buy whatever, whether it's coffee, cocktails, or a meal. I promise that no one will feel like you tricked them into a sales funnel."

I used these relationships, and the power of digital connection, to get introduced to strangers in my industry. In return for amazing conversations, I treated each person to a fun getting-to-know-you outing. During that single week in London, I made connections that have landed my business millions of dollars since. (I also came back a pant size bigger because of all of the good networking meals and drinks.)

One of my meetings was over dinner at one of Jamie Oliver's restaurants. I lunched at the Savoy and the Ivy. I met an amazing podcaster for champagne at the Goring Hotel, where Kate Middleton had her wedding preparations. At the Ritz, I had fun cocktails with 24 karat gold flakes in them. I met someone at the British Museum for tea. It wasn't a bad time.

I'm still regularly in contact with half the people I met. For example, I have taught Timothy Hughes and Adam Gray's social selling course around the world, been quoted in Tim's book, and so much more.[11] These connections are so deep that they've led to other connections—and business. Everyone else was all lovely, and I'm happy to have networked with them even if we're not in contact now.

---

11 https://www.amazon.com/*Social-Selling-Techniques-Influence-Changemakers*/ dp/1398607320

I held up my end of the bargain and never pursued anybody. This no-strings-attached connection without an expectation of sales is the signature of how I've built where I am today. Before going digital first existed, there is no generation in which I could have accomplished what I did within that single week.

The networking meetings were an investment on my part, but they've paid off immensely. It's stunning how many business and speaking opportunities that week created for me, and I learned a lot as well. I hardly talked about myself and asked as many questions as I could: What do you do? What do you like? How did you build your network? What kind of conferences do you go to? How long have you lived in London? We talked about whatever filled that hour in a meaningful way.

One conversation with a high-level strategist lasted for three hours and we had three bottles of champagne to match. Even better, we're still very good friends, and we've been on each other's podcasts. We have never exchanged money for work, but we enjoy the connection we have and rely on each other as trusted colleagues.

You have to be willing to redefine what you can get out of networking and realize that it's not all about making a sale. The thing is, no matter how many fantastic relationships you can create by going digital first, most people are too terrified to take that first step of reaching out. It can be scary, but try it anyway because they might lead to your next big collaboration.

Speed Networking

If you're not sure how to approach these conversations when you're reaching out online, say, "Hey, I'd love to give you 15 minutes and let's try to make our connection meaningful. We can meet for a cup of coffee or even hop on a Zoom call. I'll talk for five minutes, you talk for five minutes, neither of us will try to sell anything. How does that sound?" I tell my social influence students to use this strategy all the time in my online marketing strategies class.

With this approach, one student came back and said they made a $50,000 deal, even though he wasn't even trying to sell anything. That connection followed up with him later in the day and created another request to meet. Building a relationship, no matter how new, can go a long way. After all, if a connection realizes that they need your services, why wouldn't they pick you when you've built that rapport with them?

I challenge you to reach out to a few people online and use this strategy of setting up a fifteen minute meeting. I have a bespoke fifteen minute calendar link I use only for that purpose. In a sense, it's like speed networking because it's like all of the benefits of networking in a condensed amount of time.

When you've honed your ability to seek out collaboration, you can find out within five minutes if a relationship is worth your time, if you have mutual interests, or if there's something you can help each other with. Even if your help is as simple as seeing an article they would find interesting and forwarding it to them, try to be helpful and send it on. You never know where a small amount of effort into a relationship will lead.

THE GREAT EQUALIZER

I didn't come from a wealthy family. I was a missionary kid living in Spain. I went to a private Christian college and have a degree in cultural anthropology. How did I, and not a celebrity Ivy league graduate, end up on a stage in Amsterdam right before COVID speaking about digital transformation?

Because social media truly is the great equalizer. All are allowed and invited to participate, regardless of title, company, or education level. It's not hierarchical like the typical workplace.

I put it out there on the internet that I had something to say, and I got picked up as a speaker. Of course, I made good on my promise because you have to do the work, but leveraging my digital presence got me that opportunity. I didn't have the same connections that an alum from Harvard has, but I didn't need them because digital first allowed me to figure out how to make the right connections to make what I wanted a reality.

What's holding you back from reaching out to a junior staffer, saying that you really respect what they do, and asking for their help? To be clear, this isn't one-sided brain picking. In return, ask them what you can do to help them with their career. Could you pull the curtain back on senior-level positions? If they ask for specific, helpful advice in return, I can't think of anybody in the C-suite who, if someone came to us with two pointed questions and had done their homework, would say no.

Building relationships is especially important when it comes to pay equity. Many times, women tend to suffer in silos, in silence. Without having anyone to compare notes with, someone might think that $65,000 is a great salary at this place—and maybe it is, but how can she know if she doesn't realize that another company pays $39,000 for the same job and yet another company pays $109,000? Of course, you're not going to meet someone for the first time and point-blank ask them what they get paid, but you can create a trusting relationship over time that helps you understand salary and pay equity in your industry. Conversations about pay aren't taboo anymore, and many people are using the power of digital conversation to broker more equal work environments.

For some people, equity isn't about money, but opportunity. Occasionally people ask me how I became a speaker, and I tell them the same thing: I put it on my profile and website. That's it. The thing is, most people aren't necessarily concerned with how I did it, but whether I have something worthy of sharing in a speech. If you have something worthy of sharing, and you have the desire to share it, then the first step is signifying to others that you're a speaker. Opportunities will follow.

Before the internet, I had to go to every single one of those networking lunches and cocktail parties and dinners. It wasn't a hardship in terms of the food, trust me, but it was a lot of my time and investment with no clear outcome. I had no idea what I would get from any of those.

These days, we can—and should—network quickly and get more done with less, but investing in interpersonal connections is still worth it. I'm still in business with two of the guys I met on my trip to London, but it took personal effort that was strategically crafted from the digital first approach. We made one small deal that has netted me hundreds of thousands of dollars in revenue already, and by the time our collaboration is done it will probably add up to millions.

You have to go digital first and foremost, and then you can see the bigger picture of how the digital world is the great equalizer in real life.

A CLOSER LOOK: SOCIAL INFLUENCE

Digital first will grow your network, but remember this: You don't sell *to* your network. You sell *through* your network.

I talk about this all the time in my social influence course: people are not objects. When I have a meeting with someone, I'm not trying to sell him, but get to know him, and maybe eventually I can sell through him. How does this work? As I'm having conversations online with him and we're commenting back-and-forth on each other's posts, his friends are going to see me. One might ask, "Who is this Priscilla that you're friends with? She's exactly what I need." That's how you make meaningful connections and sales.

If someone wants to buy from you because they recognize your value, they'll let you know. Because everyone lives in sales avoidance mode, you have to find ways to reach those ideal customers without directly pandering to them and shoving them down a sales funnel. When you gain exposure through your digital connections, those ideal clients will think of you first when they're in the market for your services.

Once someone shows interest, you figure out how you want to work together and create a new, intentional connection. When you don't come right out and try to sell to them, you can develop a meaningful relationship.

If you're nervous about how to take the next steps, simply craft a note that is casual, but pointed. Or schedule a 15 minute meet up, as we discussed earlier.

During these calls, I always let my "guest" talk first. Often, they'll talk for the full fifteen minutes and then say, "Oh my gosh, what about you?" I say, "Don't worry about it. I'm going to write a note to connect you with so-and-so, and you can reach out to me later if you need to." I don't spend more time than my original 15 minute commitment, but I have enough information (and so do they) to know if our connection warrants more time investment.

I don't have to take my turn because I'm leading by helping. (ABH in action!) I'm not pressured to have my time in the sun, or to sell, because I don't have a scarcity mentality that says if I don't shove my pitch down this person's throat, I'm never going to get another chance to close. Instead, I have an abundance mentality that if they need me, they know who I am and my character, so they'll reach out to me. That's how meaningful connections, and meaningful sales, can create life-long relationships and opportunities far beyond a single close.

Avoid the Tribalism Trap

For this strategy to work, you have to be willing to create connections outside of your little professional bubble in which you're stuck between your boss and subordinates.

Tribalism is a bitch. It will never advance your career or your sales. You have to be interested in others, even your competition. There's no harm in saying, "Oh, you do the same thing I do over at this company. How is it? What are you dealing with? This is how I'm handling it."

Why does it only have to be job seekers who have these conversations? If you're not truly engaging with others at your level, especially those at other companies, you're missing out on opportunities for collaboration and bigger wins. There are some stingy businesses in dire need of digital help who refuse to pay for my company's digital transformation course because they're afraid of their employees getting on LinkedIn, using it well, and finding another job. To me, this insecurity is insane, and job seeking isn't wholly what LinkedIn is about anymore. And P.S.—if your employees want to find a new job, they don't need LinkedIn to do it. If your employees will leave you anyway, why not provide the value and training to incentivize them to stay?

You've heard me say it a hundred times, but it all comes back to having a sense of abundance. If you want to bring your business to the next level, there's no room for stinginess. Having the mindset of always learning, helping, asking, and listening, you start conversations, engage other people, and create opportunities for collaboration.

It's easy to get tied up in making digital connections with people who love everything you do, think exactly like you, and who have the same outlook as you. But that echo chamber isn't conducive to new ideas that could revolutionize how you work, think, or solve problems. I know it's easy to only talk to the people online who already agree with you, but it's necessary to branch out as well.

When everyone is in agreement, no one challenges the status quo, so take the initiative to create connections with the people you would normally interact with if you were standing at the water cooler and didn't have everyone's Facebook profiles a click away. Once you've created connections online—people who don't all think the same way as you—then comes the next step of connecting with them in real life.

Being online doesn't mean that you can always hide behind your screen. To create real collaborations, you can make connections online to start the process, but it's essential that you meet offline as well.

10

VICE VERSA

14 minute read

To be clear, I'm not saying that being in the same room with someone will magically lead to collaboration. See if this scenario sounds familiar:

You're excited to attend a network event and make connections. You walk into the room, look around, and realize you don't know anyone except the people you came with.

Conversations stall, if they start at all, and your questions about struggles you're facing go unspoken and unanswered. Collaborations are killed before they even have a chance to start.

If you don't know who to introduce yourself to, or how, you'll struggle to make connections. Even if you're not a wallflower, it's daunting to find the people who best align with your goals. Even if you do everything right and make amazing connections, what follows seldom varies: nothing happens.

We go to conferences with the best intentions. We meet incredible people. Then we return to our regularly scheduled lives. No one follows up, reaches out, or makes an effort to get more out of the conference. Names and faces fade, and when you run into those people at another conference, the cycle starts all over again.

If I had just one percent of the amount of money that I think business development wastes on attending conferences, I'd be incredibly wealthy. Before you throw stones at me for hating conferences, it's not the conference's fault. People work hard to create professional connections—then drop the ball or offer only one way to connect. If you don't happen to work the same way, on the same platforms, you've missed out without realizing it.

Here's what I do differently. Three weeks before a conference, I connect with every speaker on all social media and professional networking platforms. If the attendees are listed, I connect with them online as well. If they're not, I use the conference hashtag to see who is posting about their attendance. In short, I prepare.

For me, there's no such thing as a room of strangers. I walk into the room with a cheat sheet I've prepared in advance. I'm familiar with as many people in attendance as possible, and they are with me. We may not have done business together or met in person (yet), but virtually, they know me. (I'm sought after at conferences now because everyone knows about my cheat sheet. No joke, I've had people chase me down the hall asking if they could have a copy.)

I come prepared because I know that even though I'm seeing everyone in person, I've got to connect with them in multiple ways. Otherwise, I'm not going to be able to develop the relationships that will eventually turn into collaborations. You can't have a singular connection or point of contact and expect it to create a deep enough relationship to add that person in your pool, hear interesting ideas, and learn something about them. Surface-level relationships won't get you anywhere near collaboration.

When you're at a conference meeting hundreds of faces, the ones that are going to be memorable are the ones who you've been talking to already. Follow people and get them to follow you back. Follow them on all digital platforms, and then connect with them in person. This is the Vice Versa anchor that I use to establish deeper relationships more quickly and ensure they don't fall off the edge of the Earth before I unpack.

THE VICE VERSA ANCHOR

The internet is dynamic, but we create false boundaries and restrict ourselves. There are hundreds of ways to connect online, and yet we're creatures of habit. We find the platforms we like and stick to them out of familiarity.

You're probably active on more than one platform. Guess what? So is everyone else that you're connected to on that platform. Just because you found someone on LinkedIn doesn't mean that platform is their platform of preference.

That platform where you made the first connection with a potential collaborator is not their home. They probably "live" all over the internet, and they live somewhere physically too. Maybe they live in several places. You might meet someone on LinkedIn and think that's the best place to connect with them, not knowing they have a massive presence on X. If you never seek out connections on different platforms, you'll never know if a deeper relationship could be created.

True connectivity—across all platforms, venues, and situations—creates greater opportunity for collaboration. Even if you only know someone online, it's not enough to keep that relationship digital-only. People aren't trapped behind their screens. If you meet someone online, make an effort to meet them offline as well. And vice versa: if you meet them offline, connect online.

For example, in business LinkedIn is usually the best, and easiest, place to start. But it's not the have-all to end-all, and it should not be your sole point of connection. If you meet them on LinkedIn, find them on X and visa versa.

It's easier to meet people where they are than to try and get all of them to meet you where you are. Vice Versa is a way to remind yourself of this etiquette. Everyone doesn't operate at your preferred location, time, and approach. You have to be open to meeting people in other ways.

Here's another example: many younger people don't use Facebook anymore, so if you're exclusively using Facebook, you're not going to reach that younger crowd that you might need to be collaborating with. Do your research about that demographic's preferences; go on Instagram, TikTok, or another platform (because who knows what we'll all be using a year, two years, ten years from now) and connect there. Then you can connect in real life.

You might be thinking, "Wait a minute, Priscilla! You just told me I need to go digital first, and now you're saying that's not enough?" Well, you'd be right. It isn't. Just because I got you online doesn't mean you can go to your office and shut the door. Post COVID, I couldn't believe that I had known some people for nearly two years but had never met them in person. The pandemic forced us to connect digitally, but we must remember to hold space for those people offline as well.

Maybe your LinkedIn friend could also be your monthly lunch meeting buddy. Maybe they're your friend on Facebook, your follower on Instagram, and your colleague on X. People have multiple "personas," interests and accomplishments they showcase differently on different platforms. Likewise, in person they show up differently as well. Your online connections are real people, and there's so much more to them beyond their profile picture and bio statement.

Vice Versa Etiquette

Of course, every connection should begin with the Always Be Helping mindset. Chasing someone across platforms with a relentless sales pitch is an easy way to get blocked.

Social media is like a cocktail party. You can't just walk into the party, stand at the doorway, and announce, "Hey everyone! Come over here and talk to me." You have to move your legs and walk over to introduce yourself. You have to insert yourself organically into conversations at multiple venues.

The number one thing you don't want to do at a cocktail party is to walk in and loudly ask if anybody wants to sleep with you tonight. That's what people are metaphorically doing online when they contact people immediately with a business proposition or a sales pitch. It ruins collaboration because it destroys all rapport and trust. One point of contact isn't enough to launch into a request to collaborate. After all, how are you supposed to collaborate if you don't know what the other person truly needs?

I constantly get cold messages along the lines of, "I'd love to connect! Also, tell me the biggest challenge Little Bird Marketing is facing today." Why? I don't even know who you are. We haven't even had a first date.

If you want to collaborate with a competitive advantage, thinly veiling a sales pitch as an attempt to connect isn't an effective approach. It's a repellant.

Different Platforms, Different Roles

When you connect on different platforms, be conscious of your connection's likely mindset on each platform. For example, I'm a CEO, a mom, a sister, a board member, a sailing aficionado, etc. When I'm on Facebook, I'm in the mindset of talking to my mom, sharing family photos, or learning new recipes. I'm not showing up as Priscilla McKinney, CEO.

Each platform has its context: I'm more politically active on X, but I don't talk about politics at all on LinkedIn. If a connection is involved in politics or we're on a party committee together, then they should definitely connect with me on X. If not, they're missing out on key opportunities for further discussion. However, if you're trying to sell a professional service to me, then you're best connecting with me on LinkedIn. If you want to impress me, send me a handwritten note.

You already know how to make these shifts. When you attend a cocktail party, you talk about very different things than what you would at strategy meetings (and what you would discuss with your mom on Facebook). Just don't stop there. What's truly powerful is connecting in multiple ways.

Let's say that I go to a business meeting with a prospective client and we meet for lunch. Even if we had a great conversation and I write them a handwritten note thanking them for coming to lunch, that entire meeting fell flat if I don't connect with them online as well. Categorizing your contacts solely into lunch dates, LinkedIn connections, and

X friends will get you dead-end relationships. You have to do it all.

Sure, you might be used to seeing someone in a specific context, but we're all dynamic people with dynamic presences online and offline. No one exists only within the little box of their profile picture. If you go out of your way to break your mental barriers and connect with people in all ways possible, you'll create genuine connections that result in opportunities for collaboration across all platforms and situations.

It doesn't matter if you reach a person via a conference, email, snail mail, a LinkedIn message, or a X DM. Consider each situation and try something different from your initial mode of contact.

Even if you're a diehard conference attendee, you'll never see everyone at an industry conference because some people just don't attend those. Exclusively waiting until conferences to make connections means you're missing out on everyone you could reach online. There are a lot of amazing people who don't get a chance to leave the office, so to meet them you'll have to put in a little more work. But trust me, it will pay off when you realize you both have the same problems and can create an even better solution together than on your own.

Remember, this is all about collaboration. Here's a chart to help you start connecting:

IF I CONNECT WITH YOU...	I'M GOING TO CONNECT WITH YOU...
Offline	Online
On LinkedIn	On other social media platforms
Through a handwritten note	By following it up with an email
Through an email introduction	With a lunch meeting or coffee date

Find multiple ways to connect with people. Vice Versa is the anchor that puts you in more spots for more opportunities for collaboration.

VICE VERSA TIPS FOR FIRST-TIMERS

If you're new to all this, don't be afraid to jump in. If you're worried about doing it all wrong, I have some tips for you.

Don't Be Creepy

It sounds great to connect with people across all venues, but how is it done in a helpful way that doesn't come across as too forced, too eager, or too creepy?

When I write to someone online before an event, I usually say something along the lines of: "Hey! I see you're talking about XYZ. I've got that in my agenda to look into. I've got a question for you, and hopefully we'll get a chance to meet."

Mention the Connection

If I'm at an event and I get the opportunity to talk to one of the featured speakers (who are usually overwhelmed with a line of people vying to speak to them), I start with the fact that I connected with them on LinkedIn, which automatically gets our conversation off to a better start because of our familiarity with each other. Mentioning our existing online connection puts a face to the name and a real person to the profile.

Be the Vice Versa Role Model for Others

We all know the golden rule: Treat others the way you want to be treated. If you want others to inform you of their preferences, lead by example.

This is my recorded voicemail message: *Hi, this is Priscilla. I'm sorry I've missed you, I know you're busy and I am too, but I hate voicemail. So don't bother leaving me one because I won't get back to you. Text me instead.* It's true that I hate voicemail, and it's best to let them know upfront so we can connect as best as possible. If somebody texts me, I'll text them right back. But the person who continues to leave me a voicemail is the person who won't be able to connect with me on a deeper level.

Vice Versa in the Vice Versa-verse

The concept of Vice Versa even works *within* events. For example, when I attend a virtual conference, I make the most of the chat feature. After all, if we just listen and don't pay attention to our fellow attendees, are we *really* attending the conference?

In the chat, I introduce myself, ask where everybody is from, and start conversations. When I see those names pop up, I immediately connect with them on LinkedIn and say, "Hey, it's good to see you at the conference!" Back in the chat, I say, "If anybody wants to keep this conversation going on X, put your handle here so we can keep in touch. I'd love to follow you. Here's my handle."

Before we leave the virtual event, I copy and paste the chat transcript. I didn't have to leave my chair and suddenly I'm connected with a hundred people who previously would've been private and anonymous to me.

Go Live

I also take my participation at conferences and virtual events to the next level by live-Tweeting the event. For example, I'll go online and share interactions: *This is great advice from @speaker while I'm sitting here next to @attendee from @company!* Then, I'll add any relevant event or industry hashtags. On LinkedIn, I might post: *This speaker had such a great mic drop moment! This was the best reason to come to this webinar today.* I'll tag the speaker, of course, but sometimes I also tag fellow attendees and even people who aren't at the event, but who I know are interested in the topic of the Tweet. Live Vice Versa participation magnifies everyone's exposure, and it increases your social influence as well.

Of course, you don't need to Live Tweet everything. No one cares what you ate for dessert after the event. And you don't want to be Live Tweeting (or anything else) after a couple glasses of champagne. Just be aware of those moments where bringing your outside audience into an event makes sense for you and for them.

A CLOSER LOOK: THE COVETED BUSINESS CONFERENCE CHEAT SHEET

Interested in what I do before, during, and after a conference? Here's my checklist! Copy it, tweak it, and make your own cheat sheet for that next conference or event. Keep in mind it can be used for a simple virtual webinar too.

Event Cheat Sheet Checklist[12]

Three weeks before the event:

- Connect with the speakers and attendees online.

Two weeks before the event:

- Check the event hashtags and see who's already in the conversation.

One week before the event:

- Check in with the organizers. Let them know you're attending the event and see if there's anything you can contribute while you're there, such as being an event ambassador.

At the event:

- Take pictures of people's name tags and contact information so you don't forget who they are.

---

12 All free downloads created for this book can be found at priscillamckinney. com/collaboration-downloads

Hand out your business card and collect everyone's information. Have a specific list of questions and know who can best answer them.

- Share interesting conversations, insights, or facts from the event online and bring more people into the discussion, both at the event and not.

After the event:

- Reach out to the people you met online on as many platforms as you can.

- Send handwritten thank you notes.

Don't Forget the Business Cards

Have you ever tried digging through X to find someone's handle? Your business card is the perfect place to list all your social media handles and other useful information.

Did you hear that? That was the sound of someone closing my book because they think my advice about a business card is outdated. Of course boring business cards are boring, but what if they weren't?

Not only are business cards essential for recognition after the event (if you think that everyone will walk out of the conference and remember your name, you're delusional), but they're especially important when it comes to branding. When you hand someone a business card, it's a pattern interruption. You might have slipped their mind with just a verbal promise to follow up, but now they can't unsee your name. People often comment on how beautiful my business cards are, but it should be expected that I present my business well. After all, if I can't get my own branding right, I certainly can't manage a larger company's brand.

Besides physical cards, there's tech that makes sharing contact information easy. There's a special kind of event badge that I love where if you touch your badge to someone else's, it blinks green and automatically shares each other's contact information. QR codes are also a great tool for taking people directly to your website, and you can have them printed on—you guessed it—your business card. I include QR codes to my two podcasts on my business card to make it easier for someone to discover their next favorite show.

If it's daunting to try and go through all of your contacts and find them online, here's a secret: LinkedIn can do it for you. LinkedIn has a way where you can take the email addresses from your contacts, upload them, and connect with everybody in one fell swoop. You'd be surprised how many contacts people aren't connected with on LinkedIn even if they've done business together for over a decade.

CONNECT, CONNECT AGAIN, AND KEEP CONNECTING

People have different roles, personalities, and preferences about where they go, how they act, and how they connect. People show up at certain venues in a certain way. If you could connect with them at their preferred venue, magic might happen. Be open to broadening relationships by giving people the opportunity to connect in different ways that might be more their preference. When you make yourself inevitably familiar, you stand out.

It's a noisy world out there. Did you know LinkedIn reports that only one percent of people on LinkedIn actually write a personalized message when they want to connect? I'd bet even fewer are willing to connect across platforms. Having a little more awareness about how you connect automatically makes you stand out from the noise of the hundreds of connections people make both online and offline.

Really great collaboration isn't rote. It's not an obligation, and it's not a pitch, either. It has to be sincere, and taking the Vice Versa approach to collaboration creates genuine, deep relationships that are reflected in your collaborations.

11

UBER OR LYFT?

6 minute read

OFTEN WHEN I SPEAK, I'LL ASK THE CROWD, "WHO HERE IS A diehard fan of Uber? Who's a diehard fan of Lyft?" If I'm in London, I might add a black cab, or if I'm in New York, I might add yellow taxis, but you get the idea.

People will dutifully raise their hands, and then I'll follow up my survey with "It doesn't matter!" We divide ourselves into these groups, but when was the last time you got into one of these vehicles and told the driver, "Just take me anywhere you want to go"? Never. It doesn't matter which service you pick because you're in control of your destination.

Your preferred means of transportation is not relevant to where you're going, just how you got there. Similarly, you have control over where your digital preferences take you and how you use them to further your career. This is the Uber or Lyft anchor.

THE UBER OR LYFT ANCHOR

There are endless rivalries that divide us—cereal first or milk first. Top sheet or duvet only. Those who like pineapple on their pizza and those who think it is an abomination. It's ridiculous to think about, but just as you don't let your Uber or Lyft driver take you anywhere, you shouldn't let your social media preferences dictate your collaboration experience.

When you're choosing your vehicle for connection, the question isn't which one you should take, but where do you want to go? It's easy to let social media's prompts, algorithms, and interface determine your destination. Before you get yourself in a hostage situation, realize that you're still in the driver's seat.

Take LinkedIn, for example. It's true that LinkedIn is an amazing platform for collaboration, but take a step backward and realize that LinkedIn is also a multi-million dollar advertising company. Their business just happens to be connection, and they make money off people who choose their platform as a vehicle for that connection. LinkedIn directs users into particular behaviors that are profitable for the platform. I can use LinkedIn as a vehicle, but I need to be in charge of my journey.

How It Works

Let's say someone creates a profile on LinkedIn and gets 10,000 followers who are looking at her content. LinkedIn can go to McDonald's and say, "Hey, I've got 10,000 people looking at this person's content. If I sell you an ad in her content, 10,000 people will potentially look at it. What do you say?" They are getting something from you (ad space in your content) for what they offer you (a platform for that content). They need you to create great content to make this business model work.

They Don't Own You

We think we're out on LinkedIn because we're trying to connect and leverage our platforms in order to make sales, network, and advance our careers. What many people fail to realize, or what makes people not like LinkedIn, is that it can feel like a black hole. I tell people all the time to set a timer, otherwise their quick five-minute LinkedIn check can turn into hours. And that's *exactly* what LinkedIn wants.

Check Your Preferences

On the other hand, you might hate LinkedIn, but if your biggest potential client or collaborator loves the platform, then your preference means nothing. If the destination you want to reach is getting a deal closed or getting a project done, you need to be on LinkedIn too. In this digital world, missing out on a chance to collaborate because of your personal preferences means you're no longer competing. Check your preferences at the door.

LinkedIn, like all social media platforms, exists to make money. You can and absolutely should leverage these platforms to connect, but don't give them all your time. And don't be choosy about which ones you spend your valuable time on. Otherwise, someone else is going to take you somewhere you don't want to go.

We'll take a closer look now at how to steer your social media experience—and as a result, better facilitate collaboration.

A CLOSER LOOK:
SSI SCORE

Question: What is LinkedIn?

Wrong Answer: A free social media platform for business professionals.

Right Answer: A for-profit advertising arm within a technology conglomerate.

Don't get me wrong. I love LinkedIn. But I don't mistake its purpose. LinkedIn—just like Facebook, Google and down the line—creates a valuable service with a constantly improving UX/UI in order to keep people's attention longer and sell more advertising. There is nothing wrong with this business model, but before you get online, you need to understand that truth.

I teach a course on how to turn business professionals into highly respected social influencers on LinkedIn. I refer to it as the "couch potato to 5K, but for LinkedIn" course. The first thing I tell my students is that every online social platform is programmed to drive you to do the things it wants you to do. As soon as you log into LinkedIn, for instance, the platform will barrage you with prompts: *Here's this thing you need to do in your profile. Can you recommend someone? Look at this feed!*

See this promoted ad! LinkedIn will reward you for behavior that makes the platform more enjoyable for others, which keeps people there, which enables them to sell more advertising.

In fact, LinkedIn will even show your social selling index, which is a score they give you on how well you're doing on LinkedIn.[13] They'll then give you advice to raise your SSI score. That's all well and good up to a point, but we have to remember that LinkedIn wants us to do things that are good for LinkedIn because that's their priority as a business.

When we spend an hour inadvertently following prompts on LinkedIn, that's not necessarily bad or wrong. But if those actions aren't a part of our goals or strategy, then we're just letting LinkedIn drive us somewhere and we have no control over the destination. You're working for them and not getting paid—they are. In fact, you're paying them by spending your time on the platform.

In case you were curious, it is my belief that when your SSI score reaches 72 you know enough to leverage the platform for your goals and no longer need to pursue a higher score. Further work here has diminishing returns and tends to place a focus more on work for the benefit of LinkedIn—and not necessarily with a greater likelihood of reaching your goals.

---

13 https://www.linkedin.com/pulse/get-your-linkedin-ssi-score-priscilla-mckinney/

You can apply the Uber or Lyft anchor to other platforms as well. For example, I love Facebook, but if my strategy is to collaborate with CEOs, I'm not choosing Facebook as my vehicle. I'm not saying that CEOs aren't on Facebook, but when they are, they're in the mindset of talking to their mom and showing pictures of their kids. They're not in the market for thinking about B2B collaborations. If you're on Facebook, you're scrolling through and not strategizing at all because you're distracted and wasting time. You could connect with that CEO, see his posts about his kids and vacation, and still give him a sales pitch, but you're going to be blocked.

Whatever personal social media preferences you have, you need to choose the one that is going to take you where you want to go.

DON'T GET HIJACKED

You're not in a hostage situation. If you're not using the right vehicle, you're free to hop into another one. Despite the best efforts of a platform's algorithms, the last thing you want to do is develop Stockholm syndrome for the vehicle least viable for your goals.

Once you do find the right vehicle, congrats! The vehicle brought you there. But where is there? Understand where you're going so the driver can't co-opt your directions.

Simply attending the conference isn't going to do anything for you. You chose the vehicle and it got you there. You're all in Austin. Great! What now? Without direction, you'll never be able to get what you want out of that conference. Have a goal in mind, create a strategy, and know who you want to talk to and what you want to talk about. At the same time, knowing where you're going means you can recognize unplanned shortcuts to get there.

When it comes to making connections, there's always going to be some serendipity. The key is that if you only have thirty minutes to get to the destination, such as a networking meeting, you have to have a plan for how you're getting there. If the conversation takes an unexpected turn in the right direction, such as you both realize you have the same problem, then you can recognize the opportunity for collaboration and jump on it.

Now that you know where you want to be, it's time to talk about ways to make it happen. The next anchor is all about knowing what to say and how to say it.

12

RULE OF FIFTEEN

13 minute read

When my husband and I first moved to a new state and were making friends, we would go on double dates with couples we had just met. Before we left the house, I would look up a couple of jokes or funny stories in the news so I had some easy conversation topics. There's nothing worse than sitting down at a table with people you barely know and realizing you have nothing to talk about. I mean, there's only so much you can say about the weather. You can talk about yourself, sure, but for an hour? I don't care who you are—no one wants to hear you talk about yourself for an hour.

You don't need original content to start a conversation, and that's the beauty of having prompts stored away. The hardest part of any connection is starting the conversation, but once you build some rapport by sharing other people's content (those jokes and stories I just mentioned), you'll naturally find common topics to discuss.

Whenever I mention this, people who know me are shocked because I am such an outgoing person. They say, "Are you serious? You look stuff up?" Yeah, I really do because I want to show up as a good guest. After people hang out with my husband and me, I want them to think, *It's fun to go out with them. They always make an effort to include us in the conversation.*

Being prepared creates balance. If one spouse is dominating the conversation, I ask the other person questions. It's really about caring about people and leading with the ABH mindset. My approach might sound like great etiquette, but the reality is that if you want to build trust and collaborate with people, you have to first show that you are working for them.

When you go into connections with intentionality, preparation, and respect, it reflects your emotional intelligence, self-awareness, and empathy. Who wouldn't want to work with someone like that? The Rule of Fifteen anchor makes these qualities shine in your connections with others and creates the best possible opportunity for collaboration.

THE RULE OF FIFTEEN ANCHOR

When it comes to sales, many people believe that to make a significant impact in someone's buying decision, you need fifteen touches. By fifteen touches, they know who you are and what you're about.

I believe the Rule of Fifteen applies to any kind of outreach, connection, or communication you have with people—and that it's an integral part of creating the foundation for collaboration. But what does this anchor mean? It is a great rule of thumb on how to make sure you're getting the right balance of content in your online communication efforts.

Fifteen Touches by Type

To be relevant on social media and in as many social situations as possible, you must either be interesting or interested. In order to get the right mix, it's easy to curate your content or touches into these three groupings.

- Ten show you're interesting.

- Four show you're interested.

- One is your opportunity to ask for what you need or want.

People don't like being sold to, but occasionally they're looking to buy what you're selling. When they are, you want to be top of mind because of your consideration and constant contact. Being enigmatic and unnecessarily ambiguous about your profession just creates friction and doesn't land you a sale with your most ideal customer.

For fear of being salesy, many people forget to simply let others know about their area of expertise. There's a difference between humility and just not doing your job. If you're a salesperson, there's no shame in making a sale. We have real revenue goals and offer genuine value to our most ideal clients.

Shame on the person who lives on social media all the time and never asks for the sale. People show up on these platforms, especially LinkedIn, specifically as a business in a professional marketplace in order to be seen and to see what's available in business. To stay in business, we have to actually ask to do business with others. After all, we've all seen relationships end because the couple dated for more than four years without a proposal. Selling is the same when you never ask for the sale (and collaboration is the same when you never ask to collaborate).

The reason why some people's sales pitches don't work is because they neglect the Rule of Fifteen and haven't done the work to earn the right to pitch, so let's talk about what it takes to get there.

Be Interesting

When people simply curate content from other sources or create their own predictable copy without concern about how interesting it is, let's just say they don't get invited back to the cocktail party! Seriously, who wants to talk with someone who's boring fifteen times?

For every fifteen times you reach out to someone, ten of them should show that you're interesting. To be interesting online, create content that engages your audience, demonstrates perspective on a subject matter, and makes them think about something differently or question an industry standard in an interesting way.

This doesn't necessarily mean you have to be the funniest person in the room or the life of the party because this isn't about personality or how extroverted you are. It could be that you're really smart about what's going on in the industry and you have an interesting take that makes you stand out from the noise. The nice thing about being interesting is that you don't have to have to make it up yourself. Copy my dinner date strategy and collect some industry-specific conversation starters.

For example, you could mention that you read an article that said people who go to sales conferences are twenty times more likely to meet their sales goals. You can use anything that demonstrates you're interesting, experienced, and sets you apart as an authority. Having these prompts creates easy avenues for starting discussions and showing you know what you're talking about.

It's completely fine to re-use prompts, too. I have a few well-worn stories stored in my mental library that I often tell the first time I meet someone. My husband and I even have our favorite stories of funny things that have happened to us that we tell together as a couple.

No matter what stories you prepare, be mindful that you can't launch into story after story and that you've got to stop and show interest in the other person. These lead-ins are often natural, like if you talk about a book you've read and the other person brings up a related book or author. If the Rule of Fifteen is an anchor for you, you'll keep the conversation flowing without even thinking.

Be Interested

When people only think of themselves, they eventually do more harm than good. Granted, no one kicks the bore out of the cocktail party, but they do find convenient ways to extricate themselves from the conversation—and eventually the relationship. For true connection to happen, you need to show that you're interested in more than yourself.

Nobody wants to interact with someone who does nothing but talk all the time. For every ten posts, conversations, touches, or invitations—whatever it is—that are interesting, you also have to show that you're interested. Asking questions and listening is obvious, but it's also offering things in a curated way that would be interesting to them. This could sound like: "What did you do next? What are you focused on? Did you see the XYZ report that came out?" People feel cared for not only when someone listens, but when someone curates the conversation's focus around the other person.

Online, this looks like leading with downloads, articles, podcasts, or guides that are helpful for your audience. Being overtly helpful to others demonstrates your emotional intelligence and humility, builds rapport, and therefore invites comments and collaboration.

For both of these categories (interesting and interested), you can mix and match personal and professional content. As an example, your online content can be a mix of things you've written yourself and carefully curated articles written by others. While people may feel a bit awkward initially about sharing their personal life, opinions, or experiences, the truth is that social media is for humans and by humans. There's a big difference between sharing your deepest, darkest secret and simply showing that you're not a robot. After all, robots don't get invited to cocktail parties, either.

You've Earned the Right to Ask

After the first fourteen contacts, you've done the work and have the right to pitch something: "Hey, I'd love to connect with you." "Could I interview you about that book?" "Do you think you'd ever come to this webinar?" Whatever your request is, the point is that it takes time.

If you want to collaborate with someone in a meaningful way that will deliver a competitive advantage for you, you can't go in and ask them to collaborate with you as the first thing you talk about. You have to develop the relationship. If you're wondering if you're at the place yet where you can really understand what's going on with the other person and invite them to collaborate, use the Rule of Fifteen to gauge yourself.

Before you send that request, ask yourself if you've done enough work in the relationship to merit the ask. If you have, then make your ask. A lot of people don't do that; they're so shy that they'll never actually ask for the connection, dinner date, or whatever it is they want. While it might seem more polite to constantly be interested than interesting, at some point it is polite to get to the point.

If you're reading this and thinking you don't have time for fifteen touches, remember that these aren't hard and fast rules. Some organic relationships develop faster. My dad asked my mom to marry him three days after they met, and they're still together over forty years later. These anchors are simply here to help you figure out whether you're going in the right direction.

Also, you don't necessarily have to *talk* to a person fourteen times. Your touches can be both direct interactions and general online content. Simple, low-effort actions such as tagging someone on social media can count as contact. Don't overthink it. If it's too hard, you're doing it wrong.

NO EXCUSES

If you want to make connections, you have to reach out. The good news is that social media has made this easier than it's ever been.

I teach social influence for the B2B arena, and the excuse I hear most often for not posting on social media is "I don't know what to say." That excuse is followed by the close second of "I don't want to sound salesy." First of all, you *do* know what to say—you've already written tons of messages and content—you simply don't know how to curate what you have and post with the right cadence. The good news is that you have a plethora of content online to use as examples until you feel more confident finding your voice and rhythm.

If you're still unsure what to say, follow this simple rule: if you feel it, say it. Often, it can feel awkward reaching out to so-and-so or crossing the room to talk to a featured speaker. Why don't you say, "Hey, it feels a little awkward connecting with you, but it's important to me and here's why."

The reason why people don't know what to say is because they're all trying to cloak their meaning by making it sound higher-brow than it is. When it comes to collaboration, people don't trust others who are cloaking something because they can always tell. If you want to collaborate for a competitive advantage, you need to be able to trust in what it is you're really trying to say.

As for not wanting to sound salesy, the answer is simple: don't. You're a consumer too, and you know when someone is trying to ABC you. If a sales approach doesn't work on you, then why would you expect it to work on someone else? You've had a lot of conversations about sales. You know how to talk and that it's inappropriate to go in for the sale the first time. Saying you don't want to be salesy doesn't excuse you from actually making the connection.

When you're done making excuses for not connecting, and therefore not collaborating, use my anchor of the Rule of Fifteen. It's a great way to remove the anxiety and guesswork from social interaction, and it gives you guardrails so that you don't end up sounding like an ass.

On the other hand, after a nice evening of getting to know one another and experienced reciprocity, humans want to be around other nice human beings. In the end, they like to do business with nice human beings. In the quest for making what can sometimes feel awkward socially into a highly fruitful experience, the Rule of Fifteen can provide much-needed equanimity.

A CLOSER LOOK: THE PITCH SLAP

Do you remember the company that promised information on Portugal but instead dumped their potential buyers into a sales funnel? Sometimes people genuinely intend to lead with

Always Be Helping, but then they don't follow through with the Rule of Fifteen.

Say a colleague reaches out to you with an interesting article that describes current issues in the industry and what's being done about it. You're pleased and tell them so, and so they respond that they would love to collaborate sometime. Then the next day, you receive an email trying to sell their professional services to you. That's what I call the pitch slap.

Just because you led with one overtly helpful touch, or started one interesting conversation, doesn't mean you've earned the right to ask for what you want. This is baiting the other person, and it almost guarantees they won't talk to you again.

We're all busy, and sometimes even when we are well meaning, we can fall into this trap. For example, I really do want to connect and collaborate with people, but even I get anxious about getting things done. When this happens, I remind myself that the only way to build meaningful relationships is by being intentional—and that the antidote to the pitch slap is the Rule of Fifteen.

THINK STRATEGICALLY

Because collaboration is a give and get, you've got to give first. You can't sit back and wait for other people to do that. The

Rule of Fifteen ensures that you lead with giving and don't get too caught up in what you want out of a relationship.

In general, people are nervous to connect with others—and a pandemic definitely hasn't helped anyone's social skills. When people start being more strategic, not just with the work they're doing but in how they show up as a professional, they're able to actually make their goals a reality. The reason most people aren't strategic is because they go with the tide and just try to get through.

This is why I don't agree that companies should send two of their people to a conference. They inevitably hang out with each other and no one else, and they don't make any new connections. Humans tend to always take the path of least resistance—a sure method for accomplishing less than what's possible.

Do you know how easy it is to set up a committee and create a rote pattern of meeting every Tuesday? That doesn't create collaboration. Any monkey or robot can do that.

Look at the bigger picture. If you really want to have a more dynamic business strategy, more dynamic personal career strategy, and more dynamic community, you have to think strategically about every moment. That first meeting with someone is important. It teaches them how to treat you, and people rarely give up their first impression of you.

No one on my double dates thought that I had come prepared with three or four jokes, but they did walk away thinking it was fun hanging out with my husband and me. Of course, my point that night was to meet people and make friends. But if I'm going to a digital transformation conference, I'm going to read up on digital transformation and come prepared to give because my goal is to align myself with people who I could collaborate with.fee

People end up wasting their time when they go into conversations and have the mindset that they'll just see where it goes. There's always a chance that it will go nowhere, but you want to give it the best chance of going somewhere wonderful. To do this, you're going to have to curate some content, show up and ask questions, and be interesting and interested in return.

When you lead with intentionality in everything you do, others notice. You become unforgettable.

13

BE THE ZEBRA

14 minute read

HAVING A DIGITAL PRESENCE CAN FEEL LIKE YOU'RE THE main character in a robot invasion sci-fi movie. If you don't believe me, scroll through the LinkedIn connection requests you've received. Then read the ones you've sent (if you personalized it at all). Chances are, you can count on one hand the number of personalized connection messages in either column.

Never before have we had so many opportunities to connect. With a few clicks, we can connect with millions of people based on commonalities, interests, work roles, and aspirations. In fact, LinkedIn's very purpose is stated as "linking talent to opportunity at scale." We have this amazing, unprecedented opportunity, and yet people aren't making the effort to differentiate themselves from robot spam messaging.

On LinkedIn, I added a period in front of my name so I can tell when bots are trying to connect with me. If someone were to actually write me a message, they wouldn't think my name was .Priscilla (unless my parents were *very* creative). When I get a phishing message from a bot saying, *Hi, .Priscilla!* I can tell right away that it's not a real human wanting to connect with me. We might both be online, but I'm a human and I want you to treat me like one. If I'm going to connect with you, I need to know that there's a real person behind the notification willing to take a minute to greet me like they would if we were talking in real life.

I often hear people complain that LinkedIn doesn't work because they can't make meaningful connections. The thing is, it's never what they're doing but *how* they're doing it. Anyone can send a connection request—or a thousand—but how are you sending it? The definition of insanity is doing the same thing over and over but expecting a different result. So if your complaint is that it is all impersonal, then let's change that experience.

It doesn't matter how many requests you send if you don't show the basic respect of treating someone like a human being. Without that personalization, without taking the time to Be the Zebra, the request is going to get buried along with all of the other spam and bot messages.

THE BE THE ZEBRA ANCHOR

If you don't seek ways to stand out, you'll never truly be seen. In a world of horses, why not be a zebra?

When you understand the need to stand out so you can be seen and heard, you can make the meaningful connections you need for the collaborations you've dreamed about. So don't be afraid to show your stripes. This is your time to shine. To stand out. To be different. Get out there among people outside your industry and area of expertise.

If you're unsure whether or not standing out will really make a difference, take it from Gestalt theory. Let's say that sixteen people are gathered and we're all blue dots. If all of these indistinguishable blue dots are together, there's a one-in-sixteen chance that my blue dot is going to be singled out. But if fifteen blue dots are in a room and I'm a white stripe, I now have a two-to-one chance of standing out. It's math, coupled with social science.

That's why I attend conferences where I'm the only marketer. If someone has a question about marketing, who are they going to ask? I may not be the best marketer in the world, but I'm certainly the best one in that room—the most visible and memorable.

Unseen is Unsold

Being a zebra isn't about being the coolest person in the room or the most popular. Remember, being interesting means that you can have prompts instead of coming up with completely original content. When you stand out, you have more opportunities to be seen. Remember, unseen is unsold.

There's a whole industry dedicated to shopper insights, studying why people buy and the stories they tell themselves when they do make a purchase. One thing that all shopper insights experts will tell you is that product labels and shelf placement aren't accidental. Millions of dollars are spent on researching the packaging consumers reach for—what color it is, if it's sustainable, how large the text is, what font is used, if it has a full-cover label. Whether it's on the top shelf, the bottom shelf, or somewhere in between matters too. And on and on. Brands spend small fortunes trying to make their product eye-catching because they know that unseen is unsold.

What if we treated ourselves and our ideas with the same importance as logos and branding? What if you took a different approach and found a way to stand out like a zebra, then let your ideal clients—people who need what you have—approach you? When you stand out, you've actually got an opportunity to broker a connection with everyone in the room. But when you don't act, talk, or present yourself differently from anyone else in the room, you aren't going to be memorable enough. In order to create a network of people with a wide variety of expertise and opinions, you need to catch their interest.

Once you're actually seen, you create opportunities to connect with the people who can help you solve your problems. It's not just about who's in the room, either. Maybe someone's friend, coworker, or acquaintance might be the person that you need. Standing out taps into an exponential way of collaborating. If someone in the room has a former coworker who can solve my problem, they could remember me and connect us.

The Be the Zebra anchor is related to my recommendation of selling through, not to, your network. People often try to sell a product, service or idea by reaching out to one person to see if she wants it. If she doesn't, they go on to someone else—and repeat the process until they find someone who's interested. And they don't always find someone who's interested, even after many tries. (Remember what I said about insanity?)

The old sales approach was to target everyone (often one at a time, à la my LinkedIn "what not to do" guidance), and if they weren't your customer, you would undervalue that relationship and move on. There's more to that person than a potential sale because they can connect you with so many other people who can solve your problem or get you in touch with your ideal customers. This is the power of the hive mind. When you're memorable, you can find the right people to bring around a problem. And, if someone can't necessarily solve your problem, they could still figure out who can.

For example, someone might need one hundred dollars. They could go from person to person asking for that hundred dollars, and they're probably going to be turned down, but what if they asked for forty dollars? Or twenty? Maybe someone who contributes ten dollars brings in the person who can give a hundred bucks.

It's this hive mind you tap into when you expand your network, stand out, and are open about your problems. The more people that remember you, the more busy bees you have working to solve your problems. "Let me connect you with so-and-so!" "I can find that for you!" "Have you seen this article yet?" Nobody will do that for a dot in the room, but they will for a zebra over and over again.

BECOMING A ZEBRA

If standing out sounds intimidating, don't worry. There are easy ways to be the zebra, and you already know them.

If You Feel It, Say It

In the last chapter, I advised that if you feel it, say it. This is true for becoming a zebra too. Being honest is a simple way of standing out, and it's a good rule of thumb for connecting.

So few people use personal introductions on LinkedIn because they don't know how to introduce themselves or work around the awkwardness. If you feel awkward or nervous about connecting, say it. Don't get caught up in hiding your meaning by trying to make yourself sound overly professional. Honesty is a pattern interrupter in this day and age of people carefully crafting seemingly relatable, funny personable brands and then still going in for the jugular on the sale. It's as if we've learned the language of how to *seem* genuine, but something is always off.

Collaboration doesn't work when, from the beginning, one party is pretending and covering their true feelings or motivations. Case in point: "Hi, I'm so excited to reach out to you!" No, I'm not. I feel incredibly weird about all of this. Instead of fake and gimmicky enthusiasm, why don't I say, "I feel a little awkward writing to you, but it's important to me because I speak at this event and was hoping you could talk with me about this topic. Any chance we could connect?"

That honesty is a breath of fresh air, and it makes you stand out as a real person. I don't know about you, but if someone is willing to be vulnerable with me, I'll make more of an effort in return.

Start by Giving

I've said it a thousand times and I'll say it again: always be helping. Maybe the easiest way to be a zebra is to start by helping someone. I'm not saying that it needs to cost anything, but before you connect, consider what you have that you could offer someone else. This could be as simple as saying, "Hey, I noticed you have a podcast and I'm working with three people at XYZ company who are looking to be on a podcast. I'd be happy to connect you with them."

Too often our first conversation is about what I can get. *I want you to do this, click here, add me to your network, give me your opinion, let me pick your brain.* Stop expecting you're just going to continue to get without having something to give. Everyone has something to offer, and you need to be clear on what you can give before you reach out to someone.

You'll never be able to attract the collective goodwill of the hive mind if you don't have something to bring to the table. And, yes, everyone does have something that is of value to others. After all, you're not working with clones of yourself, and you have specific expertise and connections others don't have.

Maybe you have a company blog you can leverage. You could be a member of an organization and let others know how to join. Or you could make an introduction someone couldn't have gotten without a middle man.

Know How You Can Help

Sometimes, good intentions aren't enough. When it comes to offering help, how you offer it matters. It's not enough to just offer to help. Know how you can help before you ask someone how you can help. They don't know, so it's up to you to figure that out.

If someone offers to help me and it's not immediately clear how, I'm not going to look through their connections to see who I want to meet because that's a job. Instead, if that person comes to me with a specific connection in mind, they are actually being helpful. If I'm the person who needs help, why should I have to stop, recall you, ask you for help, and then show you how you help me? If you can help me, don't ask me if you can help. Just help me.

In my team meetings, everybody knows they're not allowed, at the end of their standup portion, to say, "I have some extra time. If anyone needs me just let me know." We spend a lot of money on a completely transparent project management system. If you're free, then you have time to go look and see if someone needs help and then help them. Don't wait for the busy person to come delineate what you can do for them.

Disingenuous offers of help pop up as often online as they do at funerals. People often say to someone who has just lost a loved one, "If I can do anything, just call me." I guarantee you that person is never going to make that call. While well-meaning, it's an intention of help rather than the action of it, and it makes a difference.

Actual friends don't wait for you to call. They show up at your door, leave food, clean, and do the laundry. The person who is really helpful doesn't need to tell everyone else that they're helpful. They just are. It's a matter of show, not tell.

When you set the standard, others do the same for you. You want to stand out for someone after a funeral? Don't tell them to call you if they need help. Show up and do something.

People are afraid to take that first step of giving, but no one's going to yell at you because you brought them a casserole or bought them coffee. When you're truly helping someone in a concrete way, they'll feel better, you'll feel better, and you will have stood out and made a real connection. Because when you help someone, they want to help in return. (And if they don't, they're sociopaths.)

A CLOSER LOOK:
DO NOT UNDERESTIMATE THE
POWER OF LIQUID CHOCOLATE

I travel a lot for work. When I'm going to be somewhere, I make a point to look up my LinkedIn contacts and see who's in the area. Here's the thing: I don't look for people who I can sell to. I just want to connect with people, and I make it clear that I don't expect anything in return.

On one trip to Chicago, I contacted four people, and three of them had free time for me. I mentioned to those three that one of my favorite things about Chicago is the liquid chocolate at Goddess and the Baker. None of them knew what I was talking about despite living there, so I offered to drop by their offices and bring them some.

One connection that I met with noted that she knew we were both women who had been involved in the same research group, but she didn't understand why I wanted to meet with her. I said that I just wanted to say hi since I was in town—and turn her on to this wonderful liquid chocolate. She was in disbelief that I was just there to connect and not to sell her anything. We talked for an hour and had a great conversation about books. After I left, I followed up with her by going on Amazon and sending her a book we had talked about that she wanted to read.

After our meeting, she posted on social media that I dropped by her office and brought her this liquid chocolate from a place right around the corner from her that she had known nothing about. Apparently, she was now a fan of that place too.

We didn't connect again until two years later when we were both at an event. Even though it had been years, she remembered me. She told the story to everyone as an example of how I'm just a connector—and now more people know who I am and what I'm about.

I never wanted anything from her, but I made myself memorable. To her, I'm the "liquid chocolate" lady forevermore! And now I'm memorable to everyone she tells the story to.

I went out of my way to make the connection and didn't go into our conversation with an agenda. Instead of wasting my time and effort targeting customers, I opened myself up to the possibility of an organic relationship that could develop into something more later. You have to be okay with things being unresolved and understand that sometimes relationships don't go further—but they can potentially turn into unexpected opportunities for collaboration with many more people or just accept a wonderfully memorable trip as the outcome..

Unfortunately, people often treat the digital world with the expectation of immediacy and fail to realize that this doesn't apply to digital relationships. Because they haven't been taught how to actually build relationships, they think that going online is enough. It's not. You have to be different and provide something of value.

Anyone who thinks they can broker a meaningful relationship with someone else without personalizing a word they say to them in regular society is delusional. So why do people think that depersonalization is somehow going to work in the digital world when there's even more people vying for your attention and a bigger need to stand out?

There's more to digital relationships than low-effort comments and likes. If you're online solely for sales, you might be able to scrape by with that shallow approach. But if you're in it for collaboration, you have to stand out as a real, genuine person.

INVITE ABUNDANCE

It sounds obvious, but if you're not memorable, you won't be remembered. The things that make you incredibly memorable are acts of generosity, being honest and forthright, and leading with giving. When you're always looking for a way that you can be helping, you'll naturally find opportunities for collaboration.

You never know whether a connection will go anywhere, but that's not the point. The point is to invite serendipity into your life because you never know when a quick meeting can turn into huge opportunities. That's the massive difference between forced collaboration and collaboration that creates bigger wins.

Don't limit your potential with a scarcity mindset. Look beyond what you need in a single moment. When you're willing to be in the one percent that treats others like living, breathing humans, you'll be surprised by the abundance you invite into both your life and theirs.

CONCLUSION

5 minute read

WE LIVE IN AN INCREDIBLY CONNECTED WORLD. UNFORTU-nately, we also live in a very broken world. This plays out in competition when people believe they have to compete on their own. It's me, you, them against the world. We're often like a bee that leaves the hive and forgets the power of connection to complete monumental tasks.

If we all understood the power of connectivity, and recognized the amazing resources and technology that can bring us together, we could lead a mindset shift about connections. We could successfully integrate those connections into our work, leading to collaborations so powerful that they give every one of us willing to make that leap a competitive edge.

So much in life teaches us to forge ahead on our own. What if we stopped for a minute and looked at the people to our left and right who are also trying to forge forward? Maybe instead of going alone, we could consider others in the room, the others occupying this planet with us, the people in the digital world and those in the cubicle beside us. We need to win—but they need to win, too. **Think less Queen Bee, more hive collective.**

We can, should, and really, *must* start collaborating together, as opposed to approaching the world with the win-lose attitude that holds us back. It's not a zero-sum game we're playing. I can win *and* you can win. That's the start of something. From there, we can make exponential wins happen.

The interconnectedness that technology allows is a massive opportunity for collaborating on a truly global scale. And it's not just for the generations born with a smartphone in hand. Relational, old-school salespeople have done very well on social media. They've adapted and left behind salesy messaging because they see what social media really is: God's gift to networkers and collaborators. (If you remember using a Rolodex, you understand.) Collaboration can be expansive, if only we realize the possibilities and action them.

We have to move beyond forced collaborations that are collaborative in name only. Whether you have been forced into this type of work in a committee, or by the arbitrary lumping together of people for the benefit of checking collaboration off a checklist, these collaborations are not collaborations at all; they're nothing more than working together in proximity.

We can't solve the problem with Kumbaya either. When you give up your time, money, and talent for no real benefit, that's not collaboration. It's altruism, and everyone gives but receives nothing in return. If you want to give, hats off to you, but don't confuse that Kumbaya Effect with true collaboration, or expect a competitive advantage.

We're in a new era of work where people are spearheading amazing collaborations. Brands like Truman's have found ways to change their products for bigger, more exponential wins. While these brands are vanguards of the movement toward collaboration, many have not yet taken the extra step of embracing collaboration as the new competition.

We don't have to wait for other people and other companies to lead the way. If you want to find your place in the global economy, in our new world order and new way of working, you can start your own collaboration effort to get and remain relevant and competitive.

Size does not insulate you from the need to collaborate. It's not just the little guys and disruptors who need to collaborate to stay afloat. Major brands need to sit up and listen. Collaborating for the competitive advantage is great for the individual salespeople, and it's also integral for the Coca-Colas of the world.

Use the framework, the ground rules, and the anchors to start your own collaboration effort. Did I say effort? I meant movement, because this really is a movement toward a new way of working, a new way of competing.

Always Be Helping. Look for itchy backs to scratch. Go digital—not just on one platform, but on many platforms. Go Vice Versa and get physical too. Be intentional about where your connections lead you, and which platforms you use to get there. Be interesting, be interested, and never be afraid to ask for what you want. And finally, be different. Stand out and be memorable, like a zebra in a world of horses.

The Pledge

This might feel ridiculous, but I have a request. I want you to raise your right hand and say that you will at least try to see things differently. If it helps, write a few anchors on sticky notes and put them around your office as reminders. As you're going about your day, think how an anchor could apply and how you have the opportunity to take a different approach. Could it create better collaboration? Could you engage more people? What will expand your future and not minimize it? Just try one out.

Get out of the rut that has prevented you from finding the best connections and outcomes. When faced with a challenge, ask yourself if collaboration could be a solution. If not, that's okay—you're training your internal radar so that when the opportunity comes up you won't miss it. When you open conversations with others, you're opening yourself to abundance. Bonus points if you throw your own cocktail party and try all of these anchors in one night.

If this book has changed your perspective, find ways to integrate it into your life and work. At your next conference, ask more probing questions about what people are doing, mingle with others outside of your group, and don't be afraid to strike up conversations with your competitors. Bring this book to your office and see how you can all work together to create bigger wins. Or use these fun and helpful anchor reminders at priscillamckinney.com/collaboration-anchors, starting small to build up to bigger change within your team.

Our work doesn't exist without us, so don't let outdated work structures limit your potential. After all, what is work structure but a reflection of our own personal decisions? We can sit around and play work structure all that we want, but work structure is an outpouring of our actions. We don't have to be complicit. Work structure doesn't take a seat at the meeting and impose itself on us; we decide to enforce it or dismantle it. When an opportunity presents itself for more collaborative work, we should question our structures that don't lead to the very best possible outcome for the largest group of people.

Your work matters. Your voice matters. *You* matter. Use collaboration to make the biggest impact you can, because I promise you that someone out there is waiting for the solution only you can offer—and they have something to give in return.

Keep Connecting

Now that we've connected through this book, connect with me online if you haven't already. I want to answer your questions, be your cheerleader, and hear your success stories. Use the platforms below to let me know which anchors helped you make that big breakthrough or how they're contributing to a solution.

X:

@LittleBirdMomma

@LittleBirdMtkg

LinkedIn:

linkedin.com/in/priscillamckinney

linkedin.com/company/little-bird-marketing

Websites:

priscillamckinney.com

littlebirdmarketing.com

Podcasts:

Digital Transformation Success:
digitaltransformationsuccess.com

Ponderings from the Perch:
podcast.littlebirdmarketing.com

All free downloads created for this book can be found at
priscillamckinney.com/collaboration-downloads

ACKNOWLEDGMENTS

To my parents, who showed me it is possible to carve out a unique life path, to be counter culture and yet still belong. Even though I lived in thirty-three houses along the way, they filled them each with books and taught me the importance of history and languages–the very foundations of connection and collaboration.

To three of my four older sisters, who were founding members of their created club, S.A.P. (Sisters Against Priscilla), I now acknowledge that I probably deserved the recrimination. Maybe this isn't what a book acknowledgment is about, but it seemed like an opportunity I should not pass up.

This space is reserved for some acknowledgement from my kids, Maya, Beck and Sawyer to mention that I am pretty funny, afterall. I was thinking maybe they just needed the opportunity to tell the world.

ABOUT
THE AUTHOR

PRISCILLA MCKINNEY IS THE FIFTH OF FIVE GIRLS WHO TRAVeled the world singing, in matching dresses, giving puppet shows, and going on a lot of road trips. Thirty three houses, three countries, five states, four high schools and a degree in cultural anthropology later, she has miraculously found her way into her most ideal place in the world: at the intersection of marketing, business, and market research.

Priscilla's early experiences made her curious about life, people, places, culture and the interconnectivity of it all. Intrigued by human behavior and our deep seated need to explain our often purely emotional decisions as logical, Priscilla is not afraid to ask the hard questions, a skill that serves her well as she tries to understand what makes people engage, why we buy what we buy and how we justify buying it. Whether a belief, a product or service, the human element must be understood for successful marketing.

Whether as a mom, a community leader, podcast host or a boss, Priscilla is compelled to inspire others to ask these hard questions, take risks and leave behind the status quo for the pursuit of the truth at the heart of each matter.

P.S. Don't give her caffeine. She doesn't need it.

Printed in the USA
CPSIA information can be obtained
at www.ICGtesting.com
CBHW021935020424
6252CB00002B/10

9 781544 535418